**Books are to be returned on or before
the last date below.**

Documents and Debates
General Editor: John Wroughton M.A., F.R.Hist.S.

The Rise of Labour, 1899–1951

Andrew Reekes, M.A. M.B.I.M.

Headmaster of Wells House School

First published 1991

Published by
MACMILLAN EDUCATION LTD
Houndmills, Basingstoke, Hampshire RG21 2XS
and London
Companies and representatives
throughout the world

Printed in Hong Kong

Typeset by
Footnote Graphics,
Warminster, Wiltshire

British Library Cataloguing-in-Publication data
Reekes, Andrew
The rise of Labour, 1899–1951.—(Documents and
debates)
I. Title   II. Series
324.24107
ISBN 0–333–53781–5

Contents

To Lynne, Benedict and Barnaby

General Editor's Preface

This book forms part of a series entitled *Documents and Debates*, which is aimed primarily at sixth formers. The earlier volumes in the series each covered approximately one century of history, using material both from original documents and from modern historians. The more recent volumes, however, are designed in response to the changing trends in history examinations at 18 plus, most of which now demand the study of documentary sources and the testing of historical skills. Each volume therefore concentrates on a particular topic within a narrow span of time. It consists of eight sections, each dealing with a major theme in depth, illustrated by extracts drawn from primary sources. The series intends partly to provide experience for those pupils who are required to answer questions on documentary material at A-level, and partly to provide pupils of all abilities with a digestible and interesting collection of source material, which will extend the normal textbook approach.

This book is designed essentially for the pupil's own personal use. The author's introduction will put the period as a whole into perspective, highlighting the central issues, main controversies, available source material and recent developments. Although it is clearly not our intention to replace the traditional textbook, each section will carry its own brief introduction, which will set the documents into context. A wide variety of source material has been used in order to give the pupils the maximum amount of experience – letters, speeches, newspapers, memoirs, diaries, official papers, Acts of Parliament, Minute Books, accounts, local documents, family papers, etc. The questions vary in difficulty, but aim throughout to compel the pupil to think in depth by the use of unfamiliar material. Historical knowledge and understanding will be tested, as well as basic comprehension. Pupils will also be encouraged by the questions to assess the reliability of evidence to recognise bias and emotional prejudice, to reconcile conflicting accounts and to extract the essential from the irrelevant. Some questions, *marked with an asterisk*, require knowledge outside the immediate extract and are intended for further research or discussion, based on pupil's general knowledge of the period. Finally, we hope that students using this material will learn something of the nature of historical inquiry and the role of the historian.

John Wroughton

Acknowledgements

The author would like to thank Pam Preece for all her hard work in the preparation of this book.

The author and publishers wish to thank the following who have kindly given permission for the use of copyright material:

The Earl Attlee for letter, 11 January 1945 and note, February 1943, written to Winston Churchill by C. R. Attlee; British Broadcasting Corporation for election broadcast of 5 June 1945 by C. R. Attlee; Curtis Brown Ltd on behalf of the Estate of Sir Winston S. Churchill for his 1906 Glasgow Speech. Copyright © The Estate of Winston S. Churchill; Victor Gollancz Ltd. for material from *Problems of a Socialist Government* by Sir Stafford Cripps, 1933; Guardian News Service Ltd for leader by A. P. Wadsworth in the *Guardian*, 27 July 1945; Harper Collins Publishers for material from *History of the Labour Party since 1914* by G. D. H. Cole, Allen & Unwin, 1948; David Higham Associated Ltd, on behalf of the authors, for material from *Nye Bevan and the Mirage of Socialism* by John Campbell, Weidenfeld & Nicolson, 1987, and *Labour People* by Kenneth O. Morgan, Oxford University Press, 1987; The Labour Party for material from the 1945 General Election Manifesto and the 1943 Labour Party Annual Conference Report; Random Century Group for material from *The Political Diary of Hugh Dalton*, ed. B. Pimlott, Jonathan Cape, 1986; The Joseph Rowntree Charitable Trust for material from *The Way to Industrial Peace and the Problem of Unemployment* by B. S. Rowntree, Fisher Unwin, 1914; The Society of Authors on behalf of the Bernard Shaw Estate for an extract from a speech by G. B. Shaw on 'The Ideals of Socialism', 16 February 1911; Virago Press Ltd for material from *The Diaries of Beatrice Webb Vols I–IV*, eds. Norman and Jeanne MacKenzie, 1985;

Introduction

The Labour Party is an essentially twentieth century phenomenon. The dates which circumscribe the contents of this book record the birth and rise of a working-class party to a political eminence it has never subsequently attained; in autumn 1951 Labour recorded 48.8 per cent of the vote, compared, for instance, with the 39.2 per cent achieved when it won the General Election in October 1974. It is not right, of course, to suggest that the Labour party was planned and created *ab initio* in 1900; its origins lie in the foundation of provincial labour clubs and of the Independent Labour Party (ILP) in 1893, and in the ebb and flow of trade union/employer relations in the 1890s. It was the fusion in 1899 of the two strands, of socialist political societies and of an articulate section of the trade union movement, which made the Labour Representation Commitee a possibility at Farringdon Street early in the new century. Nor would it be true to argue that there was an inevitable, and a smooth, progression in the rise of Labour. In fact, the early years were ones of strain and disappointment; Parliamentary leaders (or chairmen) struggled with a variety of negative factors. Not all trade unions joined in 1900 and the rest had to be wooed; there was a financial shortfall, especially after the Osborne Judgement; there was a persistent anti-parliamentary tendency among some which expressed itself in direct-action strikes between 1910 and 1914; it was difficult for Labour in parliament to differentiate itself from high profile Liberal progressive ministers who espoused and achieved the sort of social reform Labour itself would have introduced; and between 1910 and 1914 there was a depressing sequence of by-election defeats. Many party members and observers were concerned about the future health and identity of the party on the eve of the First World War.

For a variety of reasons, their concern was to prove exaggerated; the Liberal Party imploded with dramatic suddenness, never again to hold office after 1918. Its splits, its local disorganisation, its association with Conservatives in Lloyd George's coalition, perhaps, too, the compromises which were forced on Liberal, individual and free trading principles, destroyed the major rival to Labour on the Left. The Representation of the People Act of 1918, enfranchising the working class, undoubtedly assisted a party founded to represent the interests of that class. Labour, too, had had its splits in the war, but the party made rapid strides after 1918 and – astonishingly to contemporaries – achieved government within a quarter of a century of its foundation. However, the two Labour governments between the wars were limited by their minority status, and the steady progress towards an overall majority was rudely halted, and reversed, by the crisis of 1931. Essentially, the 1930s were spent rebuilding and reassessing; internal differences reflected the agonies which such a realistic reappraisal of foreign affairs by the leadership had upon the party. The emergence of a talented new generation of Labour politicians in this decade, to replace those either disgraced or innocent electoral victims of the fall-out of 1931, provided the basis for a recovery which continued through the Second World War. The comprehensive and – to all but a few – surprising victory in the 1945 General Election ushered in an era of radical and constructive legislation unparalleled in any other administration this century, with the possible exception of Asquith's Liberal governments between 1908 and 1912. Ministerial giants bestrode the political stage; there have been few greater incumbents of their respective offices in modern times than Clement Attlee himself, Ernest Bevin, Stafford Cripps and Aneurin Bevan.

This book ends with Attlee's electoral defeat in the autumn of 1951. That is not to suggest that that defeat signalled the end of the rise of Labour and that what followed was a steady decline into internecine turmoil, although it is a fact that the 1950s and the early 1980s have been dominated by damaging internal struggles. It is also true that the electoral base of the party, its solid trade union and working-class support, has been steadily eroded by the decline of inner-city strongholds, the collapse in trade union membership, and the growing appeal Thatcherite values of home-ownership and consumerism have had on the working classes, but, to paraphrase Mark Twain, it is clear that reports of Labour's death are an exaggeration.

Throughout and beyond the period defined by this book, certain patterns are evident. The party still bears the character which its constituent parts determined in the early years of the century; for example, important debates at the 1990 Trades Union Congress (TUC) Annual Conference were concerned with the legitimate influence trade unions should have over Labour government and the extent to which they should have most favoured status. The party fought over Taff Vale and the Osborne Judgements for its trade union paymasters; the block vote for long preserved right-wing Labour leaders in right-wing policies, especially in the time of Bevin and Deakin; trade unionists from Hardie and Shackleton to Bevin featured among the party's leaders. On the other hand, the influence of intellectual socialists within the Labour Party persists, too – in the constitution of 1918 (especially Clause 4, such a potent symbol for socialists even in 1960), in the ideas of the ILP down to 1932, and at various times with the Fabians, the Socialist League and Tribune.

From the early years of its history, there has been a tension between those members of the party wishing to offer full-blooded socialism to the British electorate, and those – usually leaders – adopting a pragmatic approach, preferring the achievement of realisable goals. Such tension was evidenced early in relations between Victor Grayson and Labour's Parliamentary leadership; it was reflected in the 1920s in the divisions between the Clydesiders, the ILP and especially Maxton and Wheatley on the one side, and MacDonald, Snowden and Thomas on the other. It lay at the root of the party split in August and September 1931; but the issue lingered on in the party and explains the differences between the Left of Bevan/Cripps and the leadership of Attlee and Bevin in the 1930s. It recurs in the 1950s in the battle between Bevanites and Gaitskell, and in the 1970s and early 1980s in the stand Tony Benn took against Callaghan and Healey. An aspect of this enduring dialogue is the debate on the means by which improvement of working-class conditions should be achieved; MacDonald strove for 30 years to establish the notion that Labour would achieve its goals through parliamentary democracy and through responsible behaviour in winning and then utilising government office. The Syndicalism of certain trade unionists between 1910 and 1914 and the General Strike of 1926 threatened this carefully nurtured parliamentarianism. Again, in the 1930s, Aneurin Bevan came perilously close to advocating direct action for his valleys constituency; and in our own times the 1984 miners' strike and Arthur Scargill's leadership represent a recrudescence of Larkin's unparliamentary principles.

Foreign policy has similarly been a controversial issue throughout the party's history. It divided MacDonald from Henderson between 1914 and 1917; it came between Lansbury and Bevin when the threat of the Fascist dictators forced Labour to reappraise its position on international matters in 1935; it led to Cripps's expulsion from the National Executive Committee (NEC) in 1939 over the advisability of a Popular Front and alliance with communists; anti-Americanism drove 'Keep Left' in 1947 to state its differences from official Labour Government policy; and the late 1950s and the early 1980s saw the Campaign for Nuclear Disarmament (CND)'s influence split the party down the middle on the issue of nuclear defence. Those tensions between socialist purists and pragmatic realists have also emerged in economic policy. They are most clearly seen in the battle between Mosley and Snowden in 1930 and essentially revolve around the degree to which capitalism, a system whose efficiency was legitimately questioned when so many of its operatives were unemployed casualties at the time, should be perpetuated by a Labour government. Labour Chancellors have, successively, chosen to run a mixed economy – even one-time radicals like Snowden and Cripps – and have been excoriated by some on the Left for their troubles.

What all this demonstrates is the considerable difficulty all Labour leaders have faced in reconciling the different wings of the party. Yet one should not underestimate Labour's unifying elements; the desire among all to improve the lot of the working class, achieve more equitable distribution, right the wrongs of the capitalist system and plan economic activity for the common good. A vision of the green uplands of a new Jerusalem, peopled by citizens blessed by fair shares for all, protected from the rude shocks of cyclical unemployment and ill-health, sheltered from capitalist exploitation by benevolent government and freed from militaristic adventurism, inspired all Labour governments to a greater or lesser extent. It was the means, and the speed at which reform took place, which differentiated Labour politicians from each other.

It is a curiosity that a party which so emphasised collective solidarity should have at the same time elevated the cult of personality. Labour history is dominated by such personalities whose decisions, inevitably, affected its course. This book, in drawing from speeches, letters, memoirs and biographies reflects the force of these figures on Labour's story. The documents serve a number of purposes; they test comprehension, they illustrate important developments, they represent particular – controversial – views about an issue and they require the student to draw on material which he/she will have to research. Together they form a chronological spine through a period when Labour grew from small beginnings to full maturity so that by 1951 there were many who believed it to be the natural party of government.

I The Early Years, 1899–1906

This chapter is concerned with the first faltering steps of the infant Labour Party, born in 1900. However, it is important, too, to trace briefly the origins of the decision made at Farringdon Street early in the century to create a new political party.

Essentially it emerged from the fusion of two elements, those of the socialist parties and of the trade union movement. Back in the early 1880s the evangelical socialist fervour of the American, Henry George, the onset of agricultural depression, the apparent dulling of the radicals' cutting edge and a new awareness of the shortcomings of capitalism in Britain conspired to awaken in a handful of middle-class enthusiasts a revived interest in socialism. H. M. Hyndman, Etonian, gentleman and former Tory, was the unlikely progenitor of the Social Democratic Federation (SDF) in 1881, a body committed to revolutionary socialism, one manifestation of which was the use of the strike to undermine the capitalist system and usher in a new and better world for the working man. The SDF, and the Socialist League of William Morris (artist and leader of the Arts and Crafts Movement) had only a few hundred members, although the influence of these pioneers was out of all proportion to their numbers. The same is true of the Fabian Society, espousing more moderate gradualist socialism (change through evolution and through permeating the other political parties with socialist ideas), founded in 1884 and boasting George Bernard Shaw, H. G. Wells and Sydney and Beatrice Webb among its leaders. The value of the two thousand or so socialist enthusiasts in these societies was as propagators of the socialist gospel.

They had a direct influence on the foundation of the Independent Labour Party (ILP) in Bradford in 1893. The ILP in its turn was to play a major part in the creation of the Labour Party proper in 1900, but it was not to be subsumed. It was to go on as a cohesive and independent socialist voice in the Labour Party into the 1930s when, led by Maxton, it was to alienate the great majority of Labour MPs. But in 1893 it was formed by the amalgamation of northern cities' local Labour clubs, the product then of provincial socialist enthusiasm. Although 'socialist' was not included in the title (to try and draw in trade union support) the party was indeed socialist, having as its objective 'securing the collective ownership of the means of production, distribution and exchange'. However, its northern base, the failure to attract London's SDF to join, and a lack of party funds, militated against the ILP's success. What was needed was to win over the trade union movement.

Throughout the period 1850 to 1880 the trade unions had been craft-based and conservative, seeing their role as that of preserving skills and standards rather than as fighting for wage rises and socialist programmes. The influence of the SDF on men like Tom Mann and Ben Tillett had a profound effect on the trade union movement in the late 1880s; New Unions, of unskilled workers, militant and socialist-led, embarked then on a rash of strikes, the London Dock strike of 1889 being the best-known example. The New Unions' membership did not amount to more than 10 per cent of total union membership, but their brief successes permanently affected Labour relations. The 1890s witnessed a series of counter-attacks by employers – Will Collison's National Free Labour Association founded to strike-break in 1893 was employed by some; and the Law Courts were drawn in to judge on the legality of striking and of picketing in the period 1896–1903, most notably in the cases of *Lyons* v. *Wilkins* (1899), which drastically limited the right of picketing by a trade union, and of the Taff Vale Judgement (1901) which rendered unions liable for damages as a result of their strike action. These employer activities alongside the creation of the Employers' Federation's Parliamentary Committee in 1898 to press in the House for legislation beneficial to the businessman, determined some trade union leaders to abandon their supine faith in the Liberal Party to press Labour's cause, and to seek instead a powerful voice in the Commons, directly speaking on Labour and trade union issues.

Not all trade unions were enthusiastic; some, like the miners and the cotton operatives, already had their own representatives in the Commons, articulating their own interests and allying with moderate Liberals to form a Lib-Lab hybrid. But it is a significant that the resolution at the Trades Union Congress (TUC) in 1899 calling for a conference of interested parties to meet early in 1900 should be put down by the Railway Servants, a new union of unskilled workers which keenly felt the brunt of the employers' offensive.

The conference which, in February 1900, determined to 'approve the formation of a distinct Labour Group in Parliament' (see Snowden document on 'The Creation of the LRC') was attended by the Independent Labour Party (ILP), the Social Democratic Federation (SDF), other socialist enthusiasts and a small – but significant – delegation of trade unionists. The marriage of two distinct bodies in the Labour movement had been achieved. This time – unlike the experience of ILP pioneers – the progress of a new Labour Party (still known as the Labour Representation Committee (LRC) until 1906) was steady and marked, even if the start was inauspicious. In the 1900 General Election, the 'Khaki' election, called in the wake of a couple of dubious British victories in the Boer War, Labour representatives were swept down in a tide of jingoism. However, the Taff Vale Judgement (see above and document of Mr Justice Farwell's decision) prompted many trade unions to recognise that only parliamentary pressure to change the law could guarantee protection from litigious employers and that that pressure could best be orchestrated by a Labour Party. Trade union membership of the LRC increased rapidly from 1902 and the engineers and textile workers (the latter, traditionally Lib-Lab moderates) were especially valuable additions.

This growth in membership, coupled with Labour by-election successes and with a certain sympathy of outlook between Mac-Donald, several other Labour leaders, and some of the opposition Liberals, helped explain the successful secret negotiations in 1903 to construct a Lib-Lab electoral pact (see documents below). Unquestionably the clear run given by Herbert Gladstone and the Liberal leadership to Labour candidates in selected seats in the 1906 election gave their party a solid foundation then. Meanwhile Keir Hardie pursued a dogged and highly individual crusade on behalf of the unemployed, caught in the trade slump of 1904–5.

By 1906 the success of the Labour Party can be gauged by the influence Labour ideas were having on some Liberals like Sir Francis Channing as well as by the direct electoral success of some Labour MPs returned to the House in the 1906 election. Yet the Labour Party was not radically socialist; the Labour Party manifesto (see document) concerns itself as much with Liberal issues like Chinese Slavery and Free Trade as with fundamentally working-class issues such as unemployment, the agèd poor and slum overcrowding. The election of 1906 was fought on the Conservative Party's record and on a Joseph Chamberlain agenda – the South African War and Protection – not on any Labour vision for the improvement of social conditions amongst working-class Victorians.

1. Beatrice Webb Recognises her Conversion to Socialism

February 1st 1890: London is in a ferment: strikes are the order of the day: the new Trade Unionism, with its magnificent conquest of the dockers, is striding along with an arrogance rousing employers to a keen sense of danger, and to a determination to strike against strikes. The Socialists, led by a small set of able young men (Fabian Society), are manipulating London radicals, ready, at the first checkmate of Trade Unionism, to voice a growing desire for a state action; and I, from the peculiarity of my social position should be in

the midst of all parties, sympathetic with all, allied with none, in a
10   true vantage ground for impartial observation of the forces at
work. Burnett and the older Trade Unionists on the one side;
Tom Mann, Tillett and Burns on the other; round about me
co-operators of all schools, together with new acquaintances
among the leading socialists. And as a background, all those
15   respectable and highly successful men, my brothers-in-law, typical
of the old reign of private property and self-interested action . . .
And then I turn from the luxurious homes of these picked men of
the individualist system, and struggle through an East End crowd
of the wrecks, the waifs and strays of this civilisation; or I enter a
20   debating society of working men and listen to the ever-increasing
cry of active brains, doomed to the treadmill of manual labour, for
a career in which intellectual initiative tells; the bitter cry of the
nineteenth-century working man, the nineteenth-century woman.
And the whole seems a whirl of contending actions, aspirations and
25   aims, out of which I dimly see the tendency towards a socialist
community, in which there will be individual freedom and public
property, instead of class slavery and private possession of the
means of subsistence of the whole people. At last I am a socialist.
From Norman and Jeanne MacKenzie (eds) *The Diary of
Beatrice Webb*, Vol. 1, Virago Press, 1984.

Questions

a   To what 'magnificent conquest of the dockers' (line 2) is
Beatrice Webb referring in this diary entry?
b   What different working-class groups does she identify in the
first part of this passage? In what sense did these elements
conflict with each other?
c   What social contrasts does Beatrice Webb draw to explain her
growing perception of the 'tendency towards a socialist community' (line 25)?
d   What are the ends of this socialist community for Beatrice
Webb?

2. The Creation of the LRC

Keir Hardie had always regarded the I.L.P. as preparing the way
for his aim of a political union of Socialists and the Trade Unions.
From the formation of the I.L.P. in 1893 he had worked quietly to
that end. The young and active members of the Trade Unions had
5   become Socialists, and they were working in the Trade Union
branches with the same object. By 1899 the time was considered
ripe to test the Trade Union Congress on this issue. Accordingly
the following resolution was put down on the Agenda of the

Congress in the name of the Railway Servants' Union. It is no
10 secret now that the resolution was drafted by Keir Hardie. I quote it
in full as a historic declaration.

> That this Congress, having regard to the decisions of former years, and
> with a view to securing a better representation of the interests of Labour
> in the House of Commons, hereby instructs the Parliamentary Commit-
15 > tee to invite the co-operation of all Co-operative, Socialistic, Trade
> Union and other working-class organisations to jointly co-operate on
> lines mutually agreed upon in convening a special Congress of represen-
> tatives from such of the above-named organisations as may be willing to
> take part to devise ways and means for the securing of an increased
20 > number of Labour Members in the next Parliament.

This resolution was carried by by 546,000 votes to 434,000
against. The majority was small. The opposition realised that this
question of Labour representation was now a practical issue. It will
be noted that the terms of the resolution did not mention a separate
25 Labour party. It left that vaguely indefinite. (In accordance with the
instructions of the Congress the Conference was called, and it met
at the Memorial Hall, London on the 27th February, 1900.)
The Trade Unions had 500,000 members represented, which was
but a small proportion of the total Trade Union membership.
30 I was present at the Conference representing the I.L.P. Other
I.L.P. delegates were Keir Hardie, J. Ramsay MacDonald, F. W.
Jowett and J. Burgess. This was the first time I had come in contact
with the Trade Union Leaders. They struck me as being a very
commonsense lot, probably quite competent at their own job, but
35 hardly the kind of men you would expect to find at the barricades
when the Social Revolution came. . . . the Conference emphatically
rejected the proposal that only working men should be regarded as
competent to represent the working class.
An attempt was made by the Social Democrats to commit the
40 Conference to a declaration that the new Party should be based on
the recognition of the class war, with Socialism as its ultimate aim.
This was an illustration of the tactlessness of the Social Democrats
which explained the reason for the failure of their propaganda to
make any impression on public opinion. At this stage to commit
45 the Trade Unions to an extreme Socialist programme would have
made the co-operation of the bodies represented at the Conference
impossible. Keir Hardie with a true appreciation of the situation,
and of the importance of carrying the Trade Unions by stages to
the ultimate goal, moved on behalf of the I.L.P. an amendment to
50 the effect that the Conference 'approve the formation of a distinct
Labour Group in Parliament whose policy must embrace a readiness to co-operate with any Party engaged in promoting legislation
in the direct interests of Labour, and an equal readiness to oppose
any Party promoting legislation of an opposite tendency'. . . .

55   It was decided that the name of the new organisation should be
The Labour Representation Committee.
        The new movement did not begin auspiciously. At the end of the
first year only 40 Trade Unions out of 1,200 then existing had
affiliated, with a membership of 353,000. The three Socialist bodies
60 had joined up. The great organisations of the miners and the textile
workers stood aloof, looking on the new movement with suspicion
and regarding it with undisguised hostility. The first Annual
Conference was held in Manchester in February, 1901, and I well
remember the feeling of despondency which prevailed. It looked as
65 if this new effort was going to share the fate of previous attempts to
secure the direct representation of Labour.
        From Philip, Viscount Snowden, *An Autobiography*, Vol. 1,
        Nicolson & Watson, 1934.

Questions

a   The 1899 Agenda resolution at Congress was the work of which
    groups of people?
b   What evidence does Snowden cite to suggest that the Confer-
    ence of February, 1900 was moderate in its intentions?
c   Why did Keir Hardie believe it to be important to be cautious,
    and which group at the Conference were considerably more
    hot-headed?
d   Why did 'a feeling of despondency . . . prevail' (line 64) at the
    first Annual Conference in February 1901?

3. Taff Vale Case, 1901: Decision of Mr Justice Farwell (*Taff Vale Railway* v. *Amalgamated Society of Railway Servants,* Appeal Cases (1901), 427 ff)

The questions I have to consider are what, according to the true
construction of the Trade Union Acts, has the legislature enabled
the trade unions to do, and what, if any, liability does a trade union
incur for wrongs done to others in the exercise of its authorised
5   powers?
        Now the legislature in giving a trade union the capacity to act by
agents has, without incorporating it, given it two of the essential
qualities of a corporation – essential, I mean, in respect of the
liability for tort, for a corporation can only act by its agents, and
10 can only be made to pay by means of its property. The principle on
which corporations have been held liable in respect of wrongs
committed by its servants or agents in the course of their service
and for the benefit of the employer – *qui sentit commodum sentire debet
et onus* – (see *Mersey Docks Trustees* v. *Gibbs* (1866) L.R. 1, H.L. 93)

15   is as applicable to the case of a trade union as to that of a
      corporation. If the contention of the defendant society were
      well-founded, the legislature has authorised the creation of numer-
      ous bodies of men capable of owning great wealth and of acting by
      agents with absolutely no responsibility for the wrongs that they
20   may do to other persons by the use of that wealth and the
      employment of those agents. They would be at liberty (I do not at
      all suggest that the defendant society would so act) to disseminate
      libels broadcast, or to hire men to reproduce the rattening methods
      that disgraced Sheffield thirty or forty years ago, and their victims
25   would have nothing to look to for damages but the pockets of the
      individuals, usually men of small means, who acted as their agents.
      That this is a consideration that may fairly be taken into account
      appears from the opinion of the judges given to the House of Lords
      in the Mersey Docks Case (L.R. 1, H.L. 120): 'We cannot think
30   that it was the intention of the legislature to deprive a shipowner
      who pays dues to a wealthy trading company, such as the St
      Catherine's Dock Company, for instance, of all recourse against it,
      and to substitute the personal responsibility of a harbour master, no
      doubt a respectable person in his way, but whose whole means,
35   generally speaking, would not be equal to more than a very small
      percentage of the damages, when there are any'. The proper rule of
      constructions of statutes such as these is that in the absence of
      express contrary intention, the legislature intends that the creature
      of the statute shall have the same duties, and that its funds shall be
40   subject to the same liabilities as the general law would impose on a
      private individual doing the same thing. It would require very clear
      and express words of enactment to induce me to hold that the
      legislature had in fact legalised the existence of such irresponsible
      bodies with such wide responsibility for evil. Not only is there
45   nothing in the Acts to lead me to such a conclusion, but ss 15 and 16
      of the Act of 1876 point to a contrary conclusion; nor do I see any
      reason for saying that the society cannot be sued in tort in their
      registered name. Sects 8 and 9 of the Act of 1871 expressly provide
      for actions in respect of property being brought by and against the
50   trustees, and this express intention impliedly excludes such trustees
      from being sued in tort. If, therefore, I am right in concluding that
      the society are liable in tort, the action must be against them in their
      registered name. The acts complained of are the acts of the associa-
      tion. They are the acts done by their agents in the course of the
55   management and direction of a strike; the undertaking of such
      management and direction is one of the main objects of the
      defendant society, and is perfectly lawful; but the society, in
      undertaking such management and direction, undertook also the
      responsibility for the manner in which the strike is carried out. The
60   fact that no action could be brought at law or in equity to compel
      the society to interfere or refrain from interfering in the strike is

immaterial; it is not a question of the rights of members of the society, but of the wrong done to persons outside the society. For such wrongs, arising as they do from the wrongful conduct of the agents of the society in the course of managing a strike which is a lawful object of the society, the defendant society is, in my opinion liable.

> *Taff Vale Railway* v. *Amalgamated Society of Railway Servants*, Appeal Cases (1901), quoted in Hancock (ed.) **E.H.D.** *1874–1914*, pp. 674–7.

Questions

a Summarise from the argument of Mr Justice Farwell here, what he deduces to be 'the contention of the defendant society' (line 16) and what the implications he foresees would be were those contentions to be 'well-founded' (line 17).

b What is the importance of the Lords' Judgement in the Mersey Docks case to Mr Justice Farwell's argument?

c What are Mr Justice Farwell's conclusions about the liability of trade unions ('societies') to legal action as a result of 'acts done by their agents in the course of the management and direction of a strike' (lines 54–5)?

d What were the implications for trade unions of Mr Justice Farwell's judgement?

★ e What was the effect on the Labour Party of the Taff Vale case?

4. The Relationship of Trade Unionism to Labour Party

If the new Labour movement were simply an attempt of Trade Unionists to use their political power for purely sectional ends – as we are told that teachers have done at School Board elections – it would be a menace to all the qualities that mark public life with distinction and honour. But when it was evident that the time had come to swing the united forces of Trade Unionism into politics, it was seen that those forces should accept allies, and take up a more commanding standpoint. Trade Unionism in politics must identify itself with something higher and wider than Trade Union industrial demands. It must set those demands into a system of national wellbeing; the wage earner must become the citizen; the Union must become the guardian of economic justice. So soon as there is a Labour movement in politics, the very meaning of Labour representation must change. The Labour representative must then satisfy more tests than that he has been a manual labourer. The narrower view was all very well so long as Labour was a mere attachment of one or other existing political party, and the Labour political movement was only an attempt to thrust workingmen candidates

upon Liberal Associations. But that was not how the moving
20 spirits of the new Labour movement regarded the work which lay
before them. Labour politics to them was the political expression of
the needs of the working class, not as a class but as the chief
constituent of the nation. The Labour problem to them was,
therefore, not merely the problem which is created every now and
25 then when Trade Unionism and Capitalism clash, but the problem
which presents itself to everyone who considers the conditions
under which Labour lives, works, is paid, dies and is buried. . . .
Thus . . . the term Labour candidate no longer necessarily signifies
a working man, but a candidate who may or may not be a working
30 man, introduced to a constituency by organisations affiliated to the
Labour Representation Committee, holding certain opinions in
politics, and believing in the Labour Representation Committee's
political method. The Committee takes its stand on opinion, not
on social status.

> R. MacDonald, *New Liberal Review*, September 1903,
> quoted by D. Marquand, *Ramsay MacDonald*, Jonathan
> Cape, 1977, pp. 83–4,

Questions

a Against what dangers is Ramsay MacDonald warning trade
   unionists in this passage?
b Explain MacDonald's arguments when he says that 'so soon as
   there is a Labour movement in politics, the very meaning of
   Labour representation must change' (lines 12–14). From what,
   to what?
c How does MacDonald see 'the Labour problem' (line 23)
   manifesting itself to 'the moving spirits of the new Labour
   movement' (lines 19–20)?
d What therefore does the term 'Labour candidate' (line 25)
   signify for MacDonald in 1903?
★ e The conflict of interest of a narrow Trade Unionism pursued by
   the payments of Labour with a wider Labour spirit was not
   confined to 1903. Does your reading of current affairs in the
   1980s suggest modern parallels?

5. The Liberal-Labour Electoral Pact, 1903

The Liberal Chief Whip's view

A determination of the course to be followed by the Liberal party is
urgently needed, for to do nothing is to seem to reject the overtures
of the L.R.C. who may be irretrievably committed to courses
during delay which they would avoid if they anticipated future
5 friendly relations.

I am keenly conscious that the matter is not so simple and clear that it may be determined in the off-hand manner in which it is dealt with by many Liberals as well as Labour men. The official recognition of a separate group unpledged to support of the Liberal
10 Party, a group which will harrass every Government and whose representatives in Parliament will probably decline the Liberal whip, is not lightly to be given. It would be the recognition of a vital change in the organisation of parties. But would it be other than the official recognition of a fact, indisputable, and clear to
15 every individual politician? There is no difficulty experienced in giving official recognition to the League group which has wealth. Why should there be difficulty in giving official recognition to the Labour group which has numbers? Neither asks for an official approval of its objects, but both seek the friendly concession by the
20 party of the liberty to run their candidates unhampered by the presence of official candidates. Are the principles and objects of the L.R.C. such as to justify such a benevolent attitude? Will the success of the Liberal party at the polls be too dearly purchased at the price? Ought the Liberal party to prefer defeat rather than assist
25 in any way to foster the growing power of the Labour Party?

These are questions the answers to which necessitate an excursus into a political discussion which it would be presumptuous of one to make. I am concerned with the electoral prospects of the party, and anxiously ask myself, 'What would be the gain and the loss to
30 the party at the General Election, if a working arrangement were arrived at with the L.R.C.?' There are some members of the party in and out of Parliament who would be estranged thereby, but they are few. Those employers of labour who remained with the Liberal party when the Whig seceders went out on the Home Rule excuse,
35 have (with few exceptions) sincere sympathy with many of the objects of the L.R.C. The severe Individualists of the party who are wholly out of sympathy with the principles of the L.R.C. are very few. The total loss of their financial aid and of their votes would be inconsiderable. The gain to the party through a working arrange-
40 ment would be great, and can be measured best by a comparison of the results of 'no arrangement' with those of 'an arrangement'.

The L.R.C. can directly influence the votes of nearly a million men. They will have a fighting fund of £100,000. (This is the most significant new fact in the situation. Labour candidates have had
45 hitherto to beg for financial help, and have fought with paltry and wholly insufficient funds.) Their members are mainly men who have hitherto voted with the Liberal Party. Should they be advised to vote against Liberal candidates, and (as they probably would) should they act as advised, the Liberal Party would suffer defeat not
50 only in those constituencies where L.R.C. candidates fought, but also in almost every borough, and in many of the divisions of Lancashire and Yorkshire. This would be the inevitable result of

unfriendly action towards the L.R.C. candidates. They would be
defeated, but so also should we be defeated.

55   If there be good-fellowship between us and the L.R.C. the aspect
of the future for both will be very bright and encouraging.

> Jesse Herbert to Herbert Gladstone, 6 March, 1903, quoted
> by P. Adelman, *The Rise of the Labour Party 1880–1945*,
> Longman, 1972, pp. 107–8.

Questions

a What disadvantage does Jesse Herbert see in the second
paragraph, of 'the official recognition of a separate group' (lines
8–9)?

b What is 'the League group' to which he refers in line 16? What
were 'its objects' (line 19)?

c What 'friendly concession' (line 19) was sought by both League
and Labour?

d How damaging does Jesse Herbert believe a working arrangement would be to members of the Liberal party?

e In what ways does Jesse Herbert go on to argue that 'the gain to
the party through a working arrangement would be great' (lines
39–40)?

6. Hardie and Unemployment

He trusted the Government would continue to do as they had
hitherto done, steer an even keel between the opposition on both
sides and pilot this measure safely into the harbour of Government
legislation. A small measure it might be, but it would mean much
5   to hundreds of thousands of men next winter and the winters to
follow. Even at the present season, with the prospects of good
trade, there were 5 per cent of trades unionists on the unemployed
benefit funds. During the summer months people managed to get a
living somehow, but the dark dreary days of winter would come
10   again, and then the number of the unemployed was always greater
than in summer. For three winters in succession municipalities and
charitable agencies had been strained to their utmost to tide the
unemployed over their difficulties, and the House should remember
that municipalities, though they might do it occasionally, could not
15   go on for ever providing relief works for the unemployed. It had
been stated that municipalities had a free hand for dealing with
the unemployed. Such talk was misleading. The powers of the
guardians were limited enough, but those of the municipalities
were nil. The only power they had was to do certain work which
20   might give employment to some of the unemployed. Seeing that
existing methods were practically exhausted it was doubly incum-

bent upon the House to back up the Government measure, in order that when winter came there should be machinery in existence for lightening to some extent the burden which fell upon decent men
25 who were unable to find employment. When they realised what want of employment for weeks and months meant to men, women, and children, not only in the present but in the future, surely Hon. Members should waive all preconceived theories spun out of the imagination of men who had been dead and gone
30 hundreds of years. He, at any rate, would not take the responsibility, by act, word, or vote, of doing anything to hinder the passage of the Bill into law. If no provision were made for the coming winter, the cursings and groanings of the hungry and the dying, the despairing, and the suicides, might well embitter the lives of those
35 who were responsible should they succeed in wrecking the Bill. It was only a beginning in the right direction, but still it was a beginning, and he hoped that the Government would stand by the position they had taken up, boldly declaring that having set their hands to this work of healing one of the gravest social sores in
40 English political life they would not be daunted by opposition, but would see to it that the Bill was placed on the Statute book before the session closed.

Keir Hardie on the Unemployed Workmen Bill, Parliamentary Debates, June 1905, Vol. 147.

Questions

a   What was the degree of seriousness of this particular rash of unemployment?
b   Which agencies traditionally dealt with the problem of the unemployed?
c   Who are 'the guardians' referred to in line 18?
d   What was the government preparing to do in the Unemployed Workmen Bill?
e   What do you deduce about the level of support for this Bill from the remark by Hardie, 'He, at any rate, would not take the responsibility, by act, word, or vote, of doing anything to hinder the passage of the Bill' (lines 30–2)? From whom was there opposition?
f   What does Hardie forecast might happen 'if no provisions were made' (line 32)?

7. A Liberal MP Speaks on Labour Issues, 1905

The corner-stone of Liberal policies should be the long-neglected group of Labour questions, which had been contemporaneously pushed aside by this Government. They had to assert the right to

live, and to live happily, the right to combine, the right of the
worker to share in determining the equitable distribution of gross
profits between Capital and Labour. . . . They had heard it said that
it was impossible for Liberalism and Labour to work together. He
had been twenty years in the Commons, and had taken a fair share
in the work of the House with regard to Land and Labour. On
every issue he could remember, where the rights of Labour were
concerned, he had found Liberals and Labour men fighting side by
side. Where was the real difference of view between Socialists and
thorough-going Liberals like himself? If it was Socialism for a State
to insist that adult men should have reasonable hours of Labour,
then they were all Socialists. He had his share on the very first
occasion that Parliament ever determined the issue of interfering
with excessive hours of adult labour, in the case of the railwaymen.
That principle was asserted for the first time by a Liberal, in the
motion as to Railway Hours he moved in 1891 and carried through
the House by a Liberal Ministry, after a Liberal had fought that
question for two years in a Select Committee of the House, and
convinced that Committee of the justice of his proposals. That
motion, which a Conservative majority had refused to accept
before, was, as soon as the Liberal Ministry of Mr Gladstone came
into power, made the law of the land.

Take 'Graduated Taxation'. Where was the difference on that?
Liberals wanted a graduated Income Tax to relieve the poor man,
absolutely fair adjustment of taxation as between one man and
another. Then Liberals, just as Socialists, wanted taxation of land
values. If Socialism meant that they should check physical de-
terioration by getting children fed properly before School, then
they were all Socialists. In that wonderful session of 1891, first
came that Liberal motion, moved by himself, to check excessive
hours on railways, defeated by only seventeen votes, two years
later made law. Then came Mr Robertson's amendment of the
Conspiracy Laws which would have prevented the Taff Vale
decision and established what nearly everybody supposed was the
legal status of Trade Unions. Another Liberal motion to secure the
rights of Labour. Then came third, Mr Sidney Buxton's resolution
accepted in a modified form by the House of Commons, to secure
the standard of 'Fair Wage' in Government contracts. That was a
great Liberal contribution to the cause of Labour. . . .

> A Speech by Sir Francis Channing, 13 September 1905,
> quoted in K. O. Morgan, *The Age of Lloyd George*, George
> Allen & Unwin Ltd, 1971, p. 141.

Questions

a How does Sir Francis Channing define 'Labour questions'
   (line 2)?

b   What example does Channing give in the first paragraph to justify the contention that 'they were all Socialists' (line 15)?

c   What further examples in the second paragraph does Channing give of Liberal concern for Labour issues?

★   *d*   How far did the Liberal government of 1906–10 enact legislation to meet these Labour priorities here enumerated by Channing?

e   Why might Channing have been making a speech like this, at this particular time?

8.   The 1906 General Election

(a)   The Labour electoral manifesto

To the Electors –

This election is to decide whether or not Labour is to be fairly represented in Parliament.

The House of Commons is supposed to be the people's House,
5   and yet the people are not there.

Landlords, employers, lawyers, brewers, and financiers are there in force. Why not Labour?

The Trade Unions ask the same liberty as capital enjoys. They are refused.

10   The agèd poor are neglected.

The slums remain; overcrowding continues, whilst the land goes to waste.

Shopkeepers and traders are overburdened with rates and taxation, whilst the increasing land values, which should relieve the rate-
15   payers, go to people who have not earned them.

Wars are fought to make the rich richer, and underfed school children are still neglected.

Chinese Labour is defended because it enriches the mine owners.

The unemployed ask for work, the Government gave them a
20   worthless Act, and now, when you are beginning to understand the causes of your poverty, the red herring of Protection is drawn across your path.

Protection, as experience shows, is no remedy for poverty and unemployment. It serves to keep you from dealing with the land,
25   housing, old age, and other social problems!

You have it in your power to see that Parliament carries out your wishes. The Labour Representation Executive appeals to you in the name of a million Trade Unionists to forget all the political differences which have kept you apart in the past and vote
30   for_____ (here is inserted the name of the Labour candidate).

From Bealey and Pelling, *Labour and Politics, 1900–1906,*
Macmillan, 1958, pp. 264–5.

Questions

a Which of these manifesto clauses would have been perfectly acceptable to Liberal and non-socialist voters?

b What, by deduction, might be the positive programme of a successful Labour Party in the next parliament?

c What did defenders of protection argue to be its benefits for 'poverty and unemployment' (lines 23–4)?

(b) Ramsay MacDonald in the 1906 election campaign

He had been across the veldt, he had seen the battlefields, the still open trenches, and it all came to Chinese labour. They were told it was going to release the slaves, the Uitlanders, to open up South Africa to a great flood of white men emigrants. They were told it

5   was going to plant the Union Jack upon the land of the free. But the echoes of the muskets had hardly died out on the battlefields, the ink on the treaty was hardly dry, before the men who plotted the war began to plot to bring in Chinese slaves. (Cheers). They could talk about their gold; their gold is tainted. (Hear, hear). They could

10 talk about employing white men; it was not true and even if it were true, was he going to stand and see his white brothers degraded to the position of yellow slave drivers? No, he was not. (Loud and continued cheers.) These patriots! These miserable patriots! If they had had the custodianship of the opinions of the country 75 years

15 ago, slavery in the colonies would have continued. When the North was fighting the South for the liberty of men, these men would have counted their guineas, would have told them how many white men had plied the lash in the southern states, and they would have said that for miserable cash, miserable trash, the great

20 name of the country required to be bought and sold. Thank God there were no twentieth century Unionist imperialists in office then. (Loud cheers).

> Leicester, 6 January 1906, quoted by D. Marquand, *Ramsay MacDonald*, Jonathan Cape, 1977, p. 94.

Questions

a What Labour and trade union issues were raised by the dispute over 'Chinese labour'?

★ *b* How far was Chinese labour an electorally important controversy?

II Labour: The Years of Promise, 1906–14

The Labour Party emerged from the 1906 elections with 40 seats, the result of the pact with the Liberal Party of 1903 and of the collapse of support for the Conservative Party, split over Tariff Reform and defensive on Education, Chinese Slavery and its lack of trade union legislation. There was, however, much consolidation still to be done for the young Labour Party. Not all trade unionists had joined the ranks of those beating a path to the new Labour Representation Committee (LRC) in the wake of the Taff Vale Judgement of 1901, and it was not until 1908 that the influential mining unions added their support to the party.

These years from 1906 to 1914 were, in some ways, ones of disappointment. True, a Trade Disputes Act reached the statute book, reversing Taff Vale and largely the product of Labour's advocacy. True, there were some extraordinary socialist by-election successes in 1907, especially that of Victor Grayson at Colne Valley, which seemed to illustrate the developing strength of labour; in fact, Grayson was a maverick, and no reliable Labour Party supporter. Critics within the Labour Movement soon pointed to the inaction and complacency of the party's leadership and indeed of the Parliamentary Party as a whole, arguing that MacDonald and others were ignoring the real issues in a slavish adherence to the policies of the Liberal Government to which they were too closely allied. One of these issues was that of unemployment, something which had concerned Hardie since the 1890s. Extracts from the writings of Tillett, the Labour leader, and Beatrice Webb, are quoted here to illustrate this. It is also true that the 1910 elections were fought on issues (Budget and Lords crisis) which were of the Liberals' choosing. Inevitably, Labour and social issues were overshadowed by the constitutional principles debated there.

Disillusion among those whom the party claimed to represent explains the 'direct action' of strikers and syndicalists in the period of Labour unrest from 1911 to 1914, whose beliefs are here explained by Tom Mann and analysed by B. S. Rowntree, and who posed a very considerable threat to the country's stability and to democratic, parliamentary socialism in these years.

The Labour Party was divided over its response to the constructive Liberalism of Lloyd George and Winston Churchill after 1908. Churchill articulates, in an extract in this section, the philosophy behind social reform, and Lloyd George made New Liberals' aspirations real both by an economic assault on those able to pay (in the People's Budget of 1909) and by his *magnum opus*, the National Insurance Act of 1911. Labour was threatened with the loss of initiative in radical reforming.

The motivation for these Liberal reforms was a complex mixture of genuine humanitarian concern and political expediency, and these Liberal ministers undoubtedly seized the radical initiative in the years after 1908. Socialists like George Bernard Shaw (quoted here) clearly saw the inevitable passage of further social reform in the aftermath to this period of Liberal innovation and warned of the skill of the Establishment in distracting radicals from their mission. The energy and imagination of these Liberal Progressives inevitably raised the punning question 'Whither Labour?'; Churchill and subsequent Liberal historians down to P. F. Clarke in 1972 saw no inevitable collapse of a Liberal Party which seemed successfully to have absorbed Labour's ranks within it. However, Pelling here, and Ross McKibbin in his *Emergence of Labour 1910–1922*, argue that, despite the unsureness of her Parliamentary performance, especially in by-elections from 1910–14, Labour was steadily growing in power and potential before 1914, with the Osborne Judgement (detailed here) only a temporary setback. For Labour members in the local parties, the issue was whether to abide by the Lib-Lab Pact which was carried from 1906 through the two 1910 elections, when Labour sustained a solid base in the Commons. By 1914 MacDonald was facing increasing pressure from local parties which wished to run Labour candidates in defiance of the central party's arrangement with the Liberals. One of the most important problems of which the student needs to be aware is the extent to which the collapse of the Liberal Party, so strong in the years before the First World War, was historically inevitable, for the rise of Labour was inextricably bound up with the electoral fortunes of its rival on the left of British politics.

1. Trade Disputes Act, 1906

1. The following paragraph shall be added as a new paragraph after the first paragraph of Section 3 of the Conspiracy and Protection of Property Act, 1875:

> Any act done in pursuance of an agreement or combination by two or more persons shall, if done in the contemplation of furtherance of a trade dispute, not be actionable unless the act, if done without any agreement or combination, would be actionable.

5

2. It shall be lawful for one or more persons, acting on their own behalf or on behalf of a trade union or of an individual employer or firm in contemplation or furtherance of a trade dispute, to attend at or near a house or place where a person resides or works or carried on business or happens to be, if they so attend merely for the purpose of peacefully persuading any person to work or abstain from working. . . .

3. An act done by a person in contemplation or furtherance of a trade dispute shall not be actionable on the ground only that it induces some other person to break a contract of employment or that it is an interference with the trade, business or employment of some other person, or with the right of some other person to dispose of his capital or his labour as he wills.

4. (i) An action against a trade union, whether of workmen or of masters or against any members or officials thereof on behalf of themselves and all other members of the trade union in respect of any tortious act alleged to have been committed by or on behalf of the trade union, shall not be entertained by any court.

(ii) Nothing in this section shall affect the liability of the trustees of a trade union to be sued in the events provided for by the Trade Union Act, 1871, section 7, except in respect of any tortious act committed by or on behalf of the union in contemplation or in furtherance of a trade dispute. . . .

Trade Disputes Act, 1906 (Public General Statutes, 6 edn, 7c 47).

Questions

a What judicial action in the previous years had prompted this new statute in labour law?

b What weaknesses in trade union law was this Act designed to eradicate? What protection did the Act now give the Trade Union movement?

c To what extent had the Labour Party been responsible for initiating and shaping this piece of legislation?

d On what grounds had an influential and articulate section of the Labour Party opposed the terms of the Act?

e What was the effect of this legislation on both trade union and Labour Party membership after 1906? Did the Act have any marked impact on labour relations in the same period?

2. Winston Churchill on Liberalism and Labour

We are often told that there can be no progress for democracy until the Liberal Party has been destroyed. Let us examine that. Labour in this country exercises a great influence upon the government.

That is not so everywhere. It is not so in Germany, and yet in Germany there is no Liberal party worth speaking of. Labour there is highly organised and the Liberal Party there has been destroyed. In Germany there exists exactly that condition of affairs, in a party sense, that Mr Keir Hardie and his friends are so anxious to introduce here. A great social democratic party on the one hand are bluntly and squarely face to face with a capitalist and military confederation on the other. That is the issue, as it presents itself in Germany; that is the issue, as I devoutly hope it may never present itself here. And what is the result? In spite of the high ability of its leaders, it has hardly any influence whatever upon the course of public affairs.

But we are told to wait a bit: the Socialist Party in Germany is only three millions. How many will there be in ten years' time? That is a fair argument. I should like to say this. A great many men can jump four feet, but very few can jump six feet. After a certain distance the difficulty increases progressively.

And here is the conclusion to which I lead you. Something more is needed if we are to get forward. There lies the function of the Liberal Party. Liberalism supplies at once the higher impulse and the practicable path; it appeals to persons by sentiments of gener- osity and humanity; it proceeds by courses of moderation. By gradual steps, by steady effort from day to day, from year to year, Liberalism enlists hundreds of thousands upon the side of progress and popular democratic reform whom militant Socialism would drive into violent Tory reaction. That is why the Tory Party hates us. That is why they, too, direct their attacks upon the great organisation of the Liberal Party, because they know it is through the agency of Liberalism that society will be able to slide forward, almost painlessly – for the world is changing fast – onto a more equal foundation. That is the mission that lies before liberalism. The cause of the Liberal Party is the cause of the left-out millions . . .

There is no necessity tonight to plunge into a discussion of the philosophical divergencies between Socialism and Liberalism. It is not possible to draw a hard and fast line between individualism and collectivism. You cannot draw it either in theory or in practice. That is where the Socialist makes his mistake. Let us not imitate that mistake. No man can be a collectivist alone or an individualist alone. He must be both an individualist and a collectivist. . . .

No view of society can possibly be complete which does not comprise within its scope both collective organisation and indi- vidual incentive. The whole tendency of civilisation is, however, towards the multiplication of the collective functions of society. The ever-growing complications of civilisation create for us new services which have to be undertaken by the State, and create for us an expansion of the existing services. . . .

I do not wish to see impaired the vigour of competition, but we can do much to mitigate the consequences of failure. We want to draw a line below which we will not allow persons to live and labour, yet above which they may complete with all the strength of their manhood. We want free competition upwards; we decline to allow free competition to run downwards. We do not want to pull down the structures of science and civilisation but to spread the net over the abyss.

> From a speech in Glasgow, 1906 published in *Liberalism and the Social Problem*, 1908, pp. 78–80.

Questions

a   In what ways does Churchill suggest that the Labour Party is better off in Britain than is the Social Democratic Party in Germany?

b   What does Churchill mean when he asserts that 'a great many men can jump four feet, but very few can jump six feet' (lines 18–19)?

c   What for Churchill is 'the function of the Liberal Party' (line 22)? In what ways does Churchill think that the Liberal Party has an advantage over militant Socialism?

d   Churchill talks much here of 'get(ting) forward' (line 22) and of 'sliding forward' (line 32). What is the goal towards which he believes Liberalism to be taking society?

e   How does Churchill reconcile traditional Liberal individualism with collectivism? What problems existed in his own party about this compromise with Gladstonianism?

f   Explain in your own words Churchill's notion of 'spread(ing) a net over the abyss' (line 57).

★ g   What legislation was passed by Churchill and the Liberal Government between 1908 and 1911 which attempted 'to mitigate the consequences of failure' (line 52)?

h   How important was the threat posed by this Liberal collectivism to the Labour Party?

3.   Ben Tillett's Faith in the Labour Party is shaken

The House of Commons and the country, which respected and feared the Labour Party, are now fast approaching a condition of contempt towards its Parliamentary representatives.

The lion has no teeth or claws, and is losing its growl too, the temperance section being softly feline in their purring to Ministers and their patronage. Those of the Party who, out of a sense of loyalty to others, refrain from protest, indicate more patience than courage in their attitude.

10 Labour is robbed of the wealth and means of life created by the genius of toil; the exploiters are on trial for their malefactions; the charge is that capitalist ownership of the land and material wealth is the cause of poverty. When that has been sufficiently explained and taught the people, there will be ample time for side issues, after the real work is done. I do not hesitate to describe the conduct of these

15 blind leaders as nothing short of betrayal, especially with the fact in view that they have displayed greater activity for temperance reform than for Labour interest. Of all the farces, these same Labour-Temperance advocates knew the bill would never pass the House of Lords; if not, they are not merely innocent but they are

20 ignorant of their own business, and cannot see an inch before their noses. Every Labour man knew the attitude of the Lords: all the Liberals did, for the game was played with the cards on the table. What a mockery it was, and merely to waste time. While Shackleton took the chair for Churchill, thousands of textile workers were

25 suffering starvation through unemployment; his ability and energy could well have been used in Manchester instead of mouthing platitudes and piffle in Liberal meetings. The worst of the winter is coming on, time thrown away will never be recovered, and thousands will perish for want of bread. A great many of the

30 victims of the destitution will be in their graves before the Liberal government will have approached the subject of unemployment, which they will sandwich between the House of Lords and Welsh Disestablishment. The temperance section, in particular, will be seizing on the other red-herrings, and the winter will have passed,

35 and these unctuous weaklings will go on prattling their nonsense, while thousands are dying of starvation. Some of these lives might have been saved to the country, the misery consequent to foodless conditions of life averted. Blessed, valuable months have been lost; the Labour movement must not tolerate the further betrayal of

40 working-class interests with agitations about the House of Lords, or Welsh Disestablishment.

> From Ben Tillett, 1908, 'Is the Parliamentary Labour Party a failure?', quoted by P. Adelman, *The Rise of the Labour Party 1880–1945*, Longman, 1972, pp. 110–11.

Questions

a Who was Ben Tillett and why would his views have carried weight with the Labour movement in 1908?

b What was the Temperance movement? What point is Tillett making about the advocates of Labour-Temperance (line 18) and about their sense of priorities in 1908?

c What was 'the attitude of the Lords' (line 21) to temperance reform, and on what grounds would Tillett have felt justified in predicting the outcome for this reform? How far can Tillett's remarks to be seen as a prelude to a greater struggle with the Lords between 1909 and 1911?

d   What for Tillett was the real issue of the winter of 1908? How fair was Tillett in condemning the Labour leadership and Liberal government for 'betrayal of working-class interests' in 1908/9 (line 39)?

★ e   What does Tillett's criticism of Labour's Parliamentary representatives say about the unity and health of the Labour movement and the strength of the party's leadership? Find out about the by-election win of Victor Grayson in the Colne Valley in 1907 and relate that to the debate on Labour's health in that year.

4.   Two Labour Views of National Insurance, 1911

(a)   The Fabian Society

Why the Fabian Society is opposed to the Bill. First and foremost because it imposes upon wage-earners what is in effect a poll-tax (i.e. a tax levied irrespective of ability to pay). The total sum to be raised under the Bill is about £25 millions. Towards this amount,
5   under the head of 'Sickness Insurance', every working man who is earning not less than 2s/6d a day is to contribute 3d a week and the State something like 1 1/2d in addition to this, every man in certain trades is to contribute 2 1/2d per week for insurance against unemployment, whilst the employer pays 2 1/2d also and the State
10   1 1/2d. . . .

To put the case in a nutshell, if Mr Lloyd George is not prepared to increase the super-tax, then he may as well give up at once his great schemes of 'social reform', for it is the most elementary of economic truths that you cannot mitigate the evils of poverty at the
15   expense of the poor.

If, as this Bill proposes, you deduct 4d a week from wages which are at present below the minimum necessary to maintain a family in mere physical efficiency, you are deliberately reducing their already insufficient nourishment, and therefore their power to resist
20   disease.

In its sub-title the Bill is described as a measure for the 'prevention of sickness', but the mere fact that it excludes all non-wage earning women and children is enough to deprive it of any claim to be taken seriously as a preventive scheme.
25   As far as the better-off workers, who are already members of friendly societies or of strong trade unions are concerned, this bill is certainly better than nothing, for it offers them solid financial

advantages which the organised section will probably be able to retain. But for the others, the comparatively underpaid, underem-
30   ployed, and unorganised, the equally emphatic answer is that the Bill is not worth having. From their insufficient incomes it takes 4d per week and in return it gives them no benefits worthy of the name.

If and when the Bill comes into force, the problem of low wages will not only remain but will be intensified. Mr Lloyd George is the
35   first Chancellor of the Exchequer who has conceived the plan of making the working classes themselves finance his measure of social reform.

> From 'The Fabian Society and the Insurance Bill', *Clarion*, 10 November 1911, quoted in Eric J. Evans (ed.), *Social Policy 1830–1914*, Routledge & Kegan Paul, 1977, pp. 178–9.

(b) Ramsay MacDonald

On the 4th of May the Chancellor of the Exchequer introduced a Scheme of Insurance so wide in its scope and so bold in its conception that even to this day we do not feel competent to pronounce on its general effect. Its foundation, however, is quite
5   simple – insurance. To this, objection has been taken on the ground that great masses of people live under the poverty line and ought not to be asked to contribute to any insurance scheme, and we have been told that the grand result of this proposal is to make the wage-earners pay towards their own sickness and invalidity the
10   enormous sum of £10,000,000 a year. . . .

We shall content ourselves with two comments. . . . The first is that the German Socialist Trade Unions, after having opposed insurance, are now its doughtiest advocates. The second observa-tion we make is that without some system of premium payment
15   the whole scheme would degenerate into a national charity of the most vicious kind, which would adversely affect wages and would not help the Socialist spirit.

> From an article by Ramsay MacDonald in *The Socialist Review*, May 1911), quoted by D. Marquand in *Ramsay MacDonald*, Jonathan Cape, 1977, p. 139.

Questions

a   What were the main proposals of Lloyd George's National Insurance Bill?
b   How did the Fabian Society think the scheme should be paid for?
c   On what grounds did it attack the Bill's proposals?
d   Why did Ramsay MacDonald support the contributory principle?
e   What can you deduce from these two extracts about the divisions on the Left of British politics over the Insurance Bill?

5.   The Osborne Judgement

Lord Macnaughten,

It is a broad and general principle that companies incorporated by statute for special purposes, and societies, whether incorporated or not, which owe their constitution and their status to an Act of
5   Parliament, having their objects and powers defined thereby, cannot apply their funds to any purpose foreign to the purposes for which they were established, or embark on any undertaking in which they were not intended by Parliament to be concerned. . . .

It can hardly be contended that a political organisation is not a
10   thing very different from a combination for trade purposes. There is nothing in any of the Trade Union Acts from which it can be reasonably inferred that trade unions, as defined by Parliament, were ever meant to have the power of collecting and administering funds for political purposes.

15   Lord Shaw,

In brief my opinion is this: The proposed additional rule of the society that 'all candidates shall sign and respect the conditions of the Labour Party, and be subject to their whip, the rule that candidates are to be 'responsible to and paid by the society' and, in
20   particular the provision in the constitution of the Labour Party that 'candidates and members must accept this constitution, and agree to abide by the decision of the parliamentary party in carrying out the aims of the constitution', are all fundamentally illegal, because they are in violation of that sound public policy which is essential to
25   the working of representative government.

Parliament is summoned by the Sovereign to advise His Majesty freely. By the nature of the case it is implied that coercion, constraint, or a money payment, which is the price of voting at the bidding of others, destroys or imperils the function of freedom of
30   advice which is fundamental in the very constitution of Parliament. *Inter alia* the Labour Party pledge is such a price, with its accompaniments of unconstitutional and illegal constraint or temptation.

Further, the pledge is an unconstitutional and unwarrantable interference with the rights of the constituencies of the United
35   Kingdom. The Corrupt Practices Acts, and the proceedings of

Parliament before such Acts were passed, were but the machinery to make effective the fundamental rule that the electors, in the exercise of their franchise, are to be free of coercion, constraint or corrupt influence; and it is they, acting through their majority and
40 not any outside body having money power, that are charged with the election of a representative, and with the judgement on the question of his continuance as such.

Still further, in regard to the Member of Parliament himself, he too is to be free; he is not to be the paid mandatory of any man, or
45 organisation of men, nor is he entitled to bind himself to subordinate his opinions on public questions to others, for wages, or at the peril of pecuniary loss, and any contract of this character would not be recognised by a court of law, either for its enforcement or in respect of its breach.

The Law Reports, House of Lords, 1910; Council of Law Reporting, 1910, pp. 94, 97, 114–15.

Questions

a   Why was this piece of case history known as the Osborne Judgement?
b   What principles as regards the relationship between trade unions and the Labour party were here enunciated by the Law Lords?
c   What was the effect of the Osborne Judgement on the Labour Party in the 1910 elections, and in the years immediately after?
d   For what reasons did the Liberal Party act to assist Labour in the aftermath to the 1911 Parliament Act? What was the nature of this assistance?
★ e   Why was legislation to reverse the Osborne Judgement delayed until 1913? What was the name of the Act, and what did it permit trade unions to do in their raising of funds?

6.   George Bernard Shaw on 'Some Ideas on Socialism'

There is no longer a division between middle class and lower class and upper class; no longer a division between Liberal and Tory and Labour; but a new division between the people who work and the people who idle. And if you want to know why it is that some
5 people speak evil of Socialism, it is because they know perfectly well that Socialism is, in the main, a campaign against idleness. Our conception is that, in the future, not a single person shall live in the country unless they EARN their living (Applause). And, although we are accused of a great many other things of which we
10 are innocent; and although you see in silly newspapers – which are the property of the wealthy classes, for it takes a quarter of a

million to start a newspaper – you see it stated that Socialism is an attack on the family and on religion; yet Socialism might attack the family and religion until it is black in the face, and not a single word to be said against it.

But it is because it has attacked idleness, and begun to insist that the enormous wealth produced by England shall be devoted to making England a better place for the people who live in it and work in it. That is the reason we are attacked, and they are very wise to attack us in this way. None of the papers can argue with me but they can only say that I have six wives and if I deny it they do not print my denial. (Applause). From Mr Keir Hardie, down to the humblest member of the Labour Party, you find almost every day that somebody in this country delivers a mass of argument, a mass of figures, and puts them very eloquently to public audiences in this country, who are convinced of the justice and rightness of what they say. But do you ever see these speeches reported in the newspapers? (Voices: 'No') No. Never one! But when you see some representative of the upper classes talking some ghastly nonsense about the Empire – (laughter) – somebody going into fits about the House of Lords or the Welsh Church, you get it at full length. (laughter). . . .

The Advance of Labour . . . Now that is what every workman in this room and outside it ought to look forward to. As I say, you are on your way to it. You have got your Labour members, and you will find your work the easier when you have payment of your representatives. . . . Only the other day they secured old-age pensions. I don't remember the exact figures, but my impression is that when you are 110 years of age you get 2s 6d per week. (laughter). In New Zealand, which is a small, insignificant and relatively poor part of this Empire, there is an Old Age Pension of 10s a week, and at a very much earlier age. Are the working classes in this country going to be content with 5s a week, which is the sum, now I come to think of it? Yes, it is 5s at the age of seventy in England and at 85 in Ireland (Laughter). Well, the working classes are not going to be content with that. They will get the New Zealand 10s, and the time will come when they may demand more expenditure on education, more expenditure on the housing of the working classes. That is to say, that since education is levied out of the local education rate – a good deal of it – since houses are built by municipalities out of the local rates, more and more money will be wanted, more and more public money. The working classes will keep pressing for it, and the upper classes, as in the past, will have to keep constantly yielding to the pressure of the working classes.

From a speech by G. B. Shaw on 'The Ideals of Socialism', 16 February 1911.

Questions

a To which body within the Labour movement did Shaw belong?
b For what reasons does Shaw suggest that Socialists are attacked?
c What power over the shaping of popular opinion do the wealthy possess?
d On what issues does Shaw allege the upper classes to be widely reported? What is he implying about the priorities of the traditional political classes?
e What signs does Shaw see of the rise of Labour in 1911?
f When were old-age pensions introduced in Britain? How correct is Shaw to suggest that '(your representatives) . . . secured old-age pensions' (lines 37–8) proposing that Labour MPs were responsible? What is Shaw's view of these pensions? What is your own assessment of their importance?
g In what sense can the final passage in this extract be seen as an exposition of the gradualism that Shaw and his fellow socialists espoused?

7.   Two Views on Syndicalism

(a)   B. S. Rowntree

Picture a young labourer with wife and three or four children dependent on him. He is of ordinary intelligence and has some acquaintance, often fairly accurate, though gleaned from fiction and the evening paper, with what life may be under more favour-
5 able circumstances. Think of him as he returns after work to the one living room of his badly furnished house, perhaps clear, perhaps the reverse, half the week redolent of washing day, the older children playing in the streets for want of a better play-ground, the younger clamouring around his wife, who is harassed,
10 anaemic, and prematurely old – although in years no older than the lovely heroine of the newspaper serial. Follow his train of thought. His wage, say 25s a week (about a third of the adult male workers in the United Kingdom receive no more, while over one-tenth have less than a pound a week), is only sufficient to pay for the
15 necessities of physical efficiency, even when work is quite regular. If he would indulge in the slightest luxury – buy his children nice clothes for the Whit Monday procession, or take his wife to the theatre or concert – he can, if he has as many as three children dependent on him, only do so at the cost of physical efficiency.
20 'The poor have no exchequer except the exchequer of the belly'.
    The children are growing rapidly, and need more food and clothes year by year. If ever he has to stay off work through illness, or loses his job, they face starvation. . . . The cheap furniture bought at marriage, is getting very shaky and will soon be

25 worthless. The clock, the china tea-service, and other simple
wedding presents were pawned when he was off work last winter
for a few weeks with 'blood-poisoning' and will never be re-
deemed. He may have spent a few pence in the week on tobacco
and beer, he may have lent a 'bob' occasionally to a mate who was
30 worse off than himself, but he can think of no extravagance with
which to reproach himself.

Perhaps our friend has attended a health lecture, and learned the
value of light and air . . . again, he may possibly have read about
the nutriment necessary to maintain the body in full physical
35 efficiency, and whether he has read about it or not, he knows quite
well that he and his are inadequately fed, in spite of all his wife's
economies. Then he reads of the immense growth of the national
wealth – from £8,548,000,000 in 1875 to £13,986,000,000 in 1905,
and sees on every hand the increase of luxury. What wonder if the
40 doctrine of discontent finds in him a ready echo? This doctrine is
preached to him by every reformer, or would-be reformer,
whether his motto be 'tariff reform and higher wages', 'tax the land
and free the people' or 'socialism and plenty for all'. As years go by,
and matters do not improve, his discontent becomes more firmly
45 rooted, and when the day comes for decision, he will be one of the
many men determined to 'down tools', even if the issue of the
conflict be very doubtful . . .

> From *The Way to Industrial Peace and the Problem of Unem-
> ployment*, Fisher Unwin, 1914, pp. 8–12.

Questions

a Why would the ideas of Rowntree expressed here have carried
weight with intellectuals, new liberals and socialists at this time?

b What would contemporaries have understood by the expression
'physical efficiency' (lines 15 and 19)?

c What privations does Rowntree's typical labourer have to suffer
to ensure mere physical efficiency?

d Why does the 'doctrine of discontent find in him a ready echo'
(lines 39–40)?

e What menu of palliatives was available to him from 'reformer or
would-be reformer' (line 41)?

f How might the discontent express itself in action?

(b) Tom Mann

What is called for? What will have to be the essential conditions for
the success of such a movement? That it should be avowedly and
clearly revolutionary in aim and method. Revolutionary in aim
because it will be the abolition of the wages system, and for
5 securing to the workers the full fruits of their labour, thereby

seeking to change the system of society from Capitalist to Socialist. Revolutionary in method, because it will refuse to enter into any long agreements with the masters, whether with legal or State backing or merely voluntarily; and because it will seize every
10 chance of fighting for betterment.

Let the politicians do as much as they can, and the chances are that, once there is an economic fighting force in the country ready to back them up by action, they will actually be able to do what would now be hopeless for them to attempt to do. The workers
15 should realise that it is the men who manipulate the tools and machinery who are the possessors of the necessary power to achieve something tangible, and they will succeed just in proportion as they agree to apply concerted action. The curse of capitalism consists in this – that a handful of capitalists can compel hundreds
20 of thousands of workers to work in such manner and for such wage as will please the capitalists. But this again is solely because of the inability of workers to agree on a common plan of action. The hour the workers agree and act they become all powerful. We can settle the capitalists' strike-breaking power once and for all. We shall
25 have no need to plead with parliamentarians to be good enough to reduce hours as the workers have been doing for a full twenty years without result. We shall be able to do this for ourselves and there will be no power on earth to stop us.

> From *Memoirs*, by Tom Mann – Labour Publishing Co., 1923, quoted in K. Benning, *Edwardian Britain – Society in Transition*, Blackie, 1980, p. 52.

Questions

a Why is the date when this was written significant in the context of British Labour relations?
b What, for Mann, are the aims of syndicalism?
c By what means would syndicalism achieve its ends?
d What is Mann's view of the past efficacy of, and future necessity for, parliamentary action to bring about reforms for the worker? Would such a view pose a threat to the Labour Party?
e Are there differences between Rowntree and Mann over the goals of working men in Britain, and the action they would be prepared to take to achieve those goals?

8.   The State of Labour in 1914

(a)   *Labour's Frustrations with the Party Leadership, 1914 – Fenner Brockway*

We protest against a cessation of activities until Home Rule is safe. Are we to forget the Government's attempts to intimidate the railwaymen? Are we to forget the Government's callous betrayal of the London dockworkers? Are we to forget the Government's rejection of a minimum of 21s a week for the railway workers? Are we to forget all the defects of the Insurance Act? Are we to forget the Government's denial of a living wage and the eight-hour day? Are we to forget the Government's broken pledges to the women suffragettes? Are we to forget the Government's surrender to the armaments ring? Must we overlook all these things on the alleged grounds that Home Rule might be endangered?

> From Fenner Brockway (ed.), 1914, *Labour Leader*, quoted in D. Marquand's *Ramsay MacDonald*, Jonathan Cape, 1977, p. 157.

Questions

a What was the strategy of the Labour leadership, outlined here, between 1911 and 1914?
b What does the language of the *Labour Leader* tell you about its view of the Government's policy towards working man?
c What does this extract suggest about the relationship at this time between the Labour Party's leaders and the rank and file?

(b) A Labour Party Demoralised? – Beatrice Webb

We attended the Gala days of the ILP conference as fraternal delegates from the Fabian Society, and listened to endless self-congratulatory speeches from ILP leaders. When the conference settled down to business the ILP leaders were painfully at variance. J. R. MacDonald seems almost preparing for his exit from the ILP. I think he would welcome a really conclusive reason for joining the Liberal Party. Snowden is ill, some say very ill, at once bitter and apathetic; Keir Hardie is 'used up', with no real faith left in the Labour Movement as a revolutionary force. The rank and file are puzzled and disheartened and some of the delegates were seen to be weeping when Snowden fiercely attacked his colleagues in the Parliamentary Labour Party. The cold truth is that the Labour Members have utterly failed to impress the House of Commons and the constituencies as a live force, and have lost confidence in themselves and each other. The Labour Movement rolls on – the Trade Unions are swelling in membership and funds, more candidates are being put forward, but the faith of politically active members is becoming dim or confused whilst the rank and file become every day more restive. There is little leadership but a great deal of anti-leadership.

> Beatrice Webb's Diaries – entry for summer 1914, M. Cole (ed.) *Beatrice Webb's Diaries 1912–24*, Longmans, 1952, p. 23.

a With what justification could Beatrice Webb 'think (that Mac-
Donald) would welcome a really conclusive reason for joining
the Liberal Party' (lines 6–7)?

b In what ways was Keir Hardie 'used up' (line 8) by 1914?

c How fair was Webb's accusation that 'the Labour Members
have utterly failed to impress the House of Commons . . . as a
live force' (lines 12–14)?

d To what positive signs does she point in asserting that 'the
Labour Movement rolls on' (line 15)?

e How serious a threat to the future of the Labour Party do you
think the weaknesses in leadership elucidated in these two
extracts to have been?

9.   A Modern Debate on the Respective Futures of Labour and Liberalism

(a)   P. F. Clarke

The electoral importance of the Labour vote can be exaggerated; it
was still an aristocracy of labour that was allowed to send its
sectional representatives to Parliament with Liberal co-operation –
– albeit one being rapidly expanded. It was Labour's propensity to
5   'grow' which has led the further inference that it would inevitably
'grow up' and 'grow out' of progressivism. But there were severe
restraints upon a party based on trade unionism. In the progressive
view, the legitimate grievances were a special case of a more
general maldistribution of resources in the community. On the
10   other hand, it was more difficult to generalise particular trade union
interests into prescriptions of society as a whole. One way of doing
so, of course, was to adopt a thoroughgoing socialist critique; but
that was hardly the formulation towards which the workingmen of
Lancashire were groping. Labour, then, could form no more than a
15   section of a party representative of the poor against the rich; it was
not of itself the true church of the working class. It fulfilled itself
after 1900, not through rivalry with Liberalism such as it had earlier
displayed, but through a co-operation that grew increasingly
close. . . . Under these conditions, it was, of all the electoral
20   pressure groups, Labour which brought the new strength to the
Edwardian Liberal revival. Despite all the shortcomings of the
arrangement, the national understanding between Liberalism and
Labour was a considerable advantage to both sides; its rupture
would have been a considerable disaster on both sides. Moreover it
25   was a more potent influence than difficulties with Liberal caucuses,
or with local socialist groups, and rendered much of the bidding
and counter-bidding for trade union support at constituency level

irrelevant. And it gave rise to a fruitful genre of progressive politics. Though Liberals might sometimes regard Labour inde-
30 pendence as the grit in the machine, it was really the sand in the oyster. . . .

The fossilised politics of Merseyside still rested upon antagon-
isms between the Trade and Temperance, between the rich and the Orangemen, between Catholics and Protestants. But elsewhere the
35 old groupings had become noticeably less important. By 1910 landed influence was important only in three or four divisions in the North West. The Roman Catholic attempt to bring out the vote in January 1910 failed miserably, and the Church of England met with an almost identical rebuff at the same time. For both churches,
40 1910 showed the limits of their power. Nonconformity rallied to Liberalism with impressive solidarity in 1906, but in 1910 was clearly no longer the dominating element in the party.

Similarly with Temperance, a dying cause even in 1906 and a dead one in 1910. Of course the old loyalties, values and prejudices
45 still had a certain pull, and there were many for whom they were still the central preoccupation. In some places, notably in Preston and in the Liverpool area, they were still dominant; but in the politics of most of the towns, the communities were disintegrat-
ing. . . .
50 Thus the first quarter of the twentieth century saw two sorts of change in British politics. The first sort centred upon the emerg-
ence of class politics in a stable form; the second sort upon the effective replacement of the Liberal Party by the Labour Party. But the first does not in any simple way explain the second. For one
55 thing, the chronology is wrong. By 1910, the change to class politics was substantially complete. That from Liberalism to Labour had not really begun. It was not a light thing to overturn one party and make another to put in its place. At the beginning of the second decade of the twentieth century it looked as though both
60 Labour and Liberalism would be subsumed in progressivism. It seemed that social democracy in England was bound up with the prospects of the Liberal Party; and in the generation after its downfall the social democratic record is not one of achievement.

From P. F. Clarke's *Lancashire and the New Liberalism*,
Cambridge University Press, 1971, pp. 339, 406, 407.

Questions

a Define the term 'progressivism' used by Clarke in line 6.
b For what reasons does Clarke believe that Labour would not necessarily 'grow up and grow out of progressivism' (line 6)?
c What, according to Clarke, was the nature of the relationship between Labour and the Liberals before 1914?

d What point does Clarke make about 'the old loyalties, values and prejudices' in the communities of the North in 1910?

e What changes does Clarke believe to have occurred in British politics in the first quarter of the twentieth century? How do his conclusions affect an assessment of Labour's prospects in this period?

(b) H. Pelling

It is easy to criticise the Labour Party of the 1910–14 period. Its M.P's were divided in their views on a number of important issues – most notably National Insurance – and they could hardly impress the observer of the parliamentary scene. Mrs Webb's view, though
5 obviously that of a dissatisfied socialist, was not really untypical.

> The Labour M.P.s seem to me to be drifting into futility . . . J. R. MacDonald has ceased to be a socialist, the Trade Union M.P.s never were socialists, Snowden is embittered and Lansbury is wild. At present there is no co-operation among the Labour M.P.s themselves nor
> 10   between them and the Trade Union leaders.

Yet the difference between the Labour Party and other political parties was that its principal strength lay in its extra-parliamentary organisation, and in this period that organisation was constantly strengthened. Between 1906 and 1914 the number of affiliated trade
15 union members rose from 904,496 to 1,575,391, with a consequent improvement of party funds. If this very largely reflects the growth of trade unionism in the country, the actual expansion of political influence is exemplified by the increase in the number of affiliated trades councils and local Labour Parties, which rose from 73 in
20 1905/6 to 177 in 1914. The number of persons elected as Labour members of local government authorities advanced from 56 in the year 1907 to 184 in 1914.

These developments occurred in spite of the concurrent development of interest in the ideas of Syndicalism and direct action, rather
25 than parliamentary methods. There is no real evidence that the 'labour unrest' of these years weakened the performance of the Labour Party in elections; and it is clear that the party's strength was increasing precisely among those workers whose younger militants had taken up with Syndicalism – the South Wales miners
30 and the railwaymen. Among the workers who were not Syndicalists nor even Socialists – and they were still by far the majority – a sort of undogmatic 'Labourism' was establishing itself, which consisted in little more than the opinion that the Labour Party, and not the Liberal, was the party for working men to belong to. This
35 was of course particularly the case now with the miners, whose political solidarity was unmatched by other occupational groups.

Sooner or later – and there were indications that it would be sooner – the remnant of Liberalism among the Midland miners would be eliminated and they would be brought into line with their English, Welsh and Scottish fellows.

40

> From H. Pelling's 'Labour and the Downfall of Liberalism', published in *Popular Politics and Society in Late Victorian Britain*, Macmillan, 1968, pp. 117–18.

Questions

a What criticisms of the party between 1910 and 1914 does Pelling accept can be made about Labour?

b What does he believe to be the principal strength of the Labour Party *vis-à-vis* the other political parties?

★ c How serious a danger does Pelling believe syndicalism to have been to the Labour Party in this period? From your own reading, and from extracts in this chapter, would you accept his evaluation?

d Define Pelling's 'undogmatic Labourism' (line 32).

e Compare Clarke and Pelling's estimation of the Labour Party's prospects in 1914. Had a major and destructive war not broken out in 1914, could the Liberal Party have prevented the seemingly inexorable rise of Labour?

III   Labour's War and its Aftermath, 1914–24

The war in August 1914 was to split the Labour Party just as it split its Liberal rivals. But whereas the Liberals were riven irrevocably, especially by divisions between Asquith and Lloyd George, the Labour Party somehow retained a tenuous unity from 1914 to 1917, at a time when its members either supported the war wholeheartedly, opposed this particular war as being caused as much by secret diplomacy and British Imperial ambition as by German expansionism, or took an uncompromisingly pacifist position (see Beatrice Webb). Ramsay MacDonald, Labour's pre-war Chairman, resigned from his leadership because he adhered to the middle of these three positions and found his party comprehensively outnumbering him. A minority of Labour MPs fought hard over issues like the extension of conscription and the adhesion of Labour men to Lloyd George's new administration in 1916 (see passages by Snowden and Webb below), but the trade union and Henderson line of support for the prosecution of the war prevailed until the fall-out from the February 1917 Revolution in Russia drove Henderson from the Cabinet and united Labour once again around the policy of a democratically negotiated peace, an end to working-class sacrifice, and a rejection of the notion that war could only terminate with conquest and occupation of the enemies' lands. Labour was in the forefront of articulating constructive war aims and positive thinking about the make-up of a post-war world.

Henderson's resignation from the Lloyd George administration over the Prime Minister's unwillingness to countenance Labour representation at the Stockholm Conference of Socialist Parties (including German) led him to plan far-sightedly for Labour's domestic political future. He and Sidney Webb devised a new constitution for the party which was adopted at a Special Conference in February 1918. This constitution embodied a statement of policy aims which were overtly socialist and espoused, for instance, the common ownership of the means of production and the best obtainable system of popular administration and control of each industry and service (the infamous Clause 4); it also, and with more immediate impact, turned the pre-war loose-knit labour alliance into a national party with a mass membership and a network of local branches, whilst at the same time it consolidated the political power of the trade unions whose block votes now overwhelmed those of socialist societies at Party Conferences.

The new organisation was still incomplete when the war ended and Lloyd George called his Coupon Election. Electoral euphoria engendered by victory ensured a handsome government majority, and Labour won only 57 seats, with national leaders like MacDonald, Snowden and Henderson defeated in the backlash against those who had dared to oppose the conduct of the war. Beatrice Webb amusingly records Labour's position in the aftermath to the election. MacDonald, Jowett and others proved to have been prescient about Versailles but in truth the party remained a movement full of fissures between trade unions and the Independent Labour Party (ILP), intellectuals and workers, pacifists and patriots, and direct-action left-wingers and parliamentarian right-wingers. The depressing aftermath to the post-war boom encouraged those who propounded Moscow-inspired revolution or who looked to the strike to usher in the socialist Jerusalem. One group made up of Marxists, communists or municipal socialists was that of the Clydesiders, Glasgow Labour politicians, some of whom were suspected of planning revolution in that city in 1919, and some of whom were to be voted into the Commons in the December 1923 Election.

Suspicion of treasonable activity concerned the authorities and their intelligence agents (see the report of one such agent below). Labour leaders like Henderson fought hard to preserve the party's independence of communists, despite the ILP's flirtation with Moscow throughout the early 1920s. MacDonald, who was to emerge as Labour leader in 1922 after winning his way back to Westminster through the Aberavon constituency, sought to present Labour as a sober, realistic and responsible opposition to the Conservative Party. The result of the 1922 General Election won by Bonar Law's Conservatives saw Labour the leading party of the left with 142 seats and opened up the giddy prospect of power for a party only as old as the youthful century itself. So notorious behaviour like that of Maxton and other left-wingers in July 1923 in employing inflammatory language and attitudes of intransigent class war embarrassed the centre and right of the Labour Party.

Baldwin, who had succeeded the dying Bonar Law as Prime Minister in early 1923, surprisingly called a General Election on the issue of Protection in October of that year.

But the outcome was a defeat for Baldwin whose party remained the largest in the Commons, but which had no overall majority over Labour (191 seats) and the recently reunited Liberals (146 seats). The Labour ranks had been swelled by the phalanx of Glaswegians, the Clydesiders, who had an almost religious sense of mission and a thoroughly uncompromising determination not to be deflected from their goal by the clubbable seductiveness of Westminster.

Baldwin's recognition that the Conservatives had failed to win a mandate for Protection, and Asquith's belief that if the country was to experiment with a Labour administration now was as safe a time as any, led to the King's offer to MacDonald to form a government, which he did successfully in January 1924.

1. War and Socialists

3rd May (41 Grosvenor Road)

The Inner Circle of the Fabian Society is distinguished for the intensity of the difference of opinion with regard to the cause of the war and the right way of ending it. Clifford Allen, the youngest member of the Executive, is a fanatical anti-war pro-German
5 advocate who distorts every fact to prove his country wrong. Ensor, one of the most accomplished of the middle-aged members, is complacently convinced of the imperative need not only of beating Germany but of dismembering the German empire, of setting up Hungary and the Slav provinces of Austria as indepen-
10 dent states, whilst adding south Germany to a Germanized Austria! Prussian Germany is to be stripped of her colonies and compelled to disarm. Sidney is just the same British patriot repudiating any attempt to dismember or humiliate the German people and intent on a brave attempt, engineered by Great Britain and the U.S.A. to
15 establish a supernational control over all the states alike. Sanders agrees, but is more distinctly anti-German. The bulk of the members follow Sidney, but there is a small but intense section of pacifists. The Guild Socialists would be pro-war if they were not in rebellion against the government on principle, and if they did not
20 hate the thought of fighting themselves, being hedonists.

The junta that control I.L.P. are vehement pacifists, the leading men of the British Socialist Party violent anti-German patriots. The ruck of the trade union officials are just sane and commonplace supporters of the British government against its enemies.
25 The war has developed the antagonism between the Parliamentary Labour Party and the I.L.P. almost to a breaking point, the latter being now in close communion with the sentimental Whigs of the Arthur Ponsonby-C.P. Trevelyan-Courtney type, whilst there is a distinct increase of friendliness between the 'Front Bench'
30 of the Fabian Society, and the Parliamentary Labour Party. Perhaps the most noted result is the consciousness of world failure on the part of the international labour and socialist movement, a consciousness of a certain self-deception – all fine talk, all our glowing shibboleths are proved to be mere surface froth. . . . And oddly

35   enough, there is, at present, no anger with them. There is no jingo
      mob. There is a section of the working class who are slacking and
      drinking, who, like the army contractors, are making the country's
      need the opportunity for exactions, but there is no popular
      anti-pacifist feeling. . . . The criminal classes are the only ones to
40   visibly improve the character. They have given up crime and
      enlisted in large numbers. The women of all classes have emerged
      into public life – industrial, social and militarist. . . .

> Beatrice Webb's Diaries, entry for 3 May 1915, Norman and
> Jeanne MacKenzie (eds) *The Diary of Beatrice Webb*, Virago
> Press, 1984.

Questions

a   In what ways do the divisions in the Fabian Society described
    here by Beatrice Webb reflect the division within the Labour
    Party at large?
b   What were the respective positions of the Parliamentary Labour
    Party and the I.L.P. on the issue of the war?
c   In what sense does Beatrice Webb talk of 'a consciousness of
    world failure on the part of international labour' (lines 31–2)?
d   What does she believe are the reactions of the working class
    towards war (lines 35–41)?

2.   Snowden on Conscription

It seems to me – I am no military expert – that if we want to win by
fighting we ought to concentrate all our available resources upon
getting an enormous superiority in munitions, and if we are going
to follow the policy proposed in this Bill that is going to be an
5   impossible thing to do.
      So far as the conscriptionist members of the Government are
concerned, I declare it as my firm conviction that their main reason
for support of this Bill is not on account of military necessity, but
because it is going to put into their hands a strong weapon for
10   enforcing the chains of slavery on democracy. . . . This Bill is just a
repetition of what occurred during the Napoleonic Wars. . . . The
Conspiracy Acts were passed, and it took the working people of
this country fifty years to recover the liberties which were taken
away from them during that time.
15   It certainly does not lie in the mouths of Members opposite to
charge us with want of patriotism. If it be unpatriotic not to
approve when the rights and liberties of the people are being taken
away, then I am no patriot, but I refuse to have my patriotism
judged by the patriotism of Honourable Members opposite. Some
20   of us have spent the greater part of a lifetime – (An Hon. Member:

'In upsetting the country'.) We have evidently succeeded in upsetting Honourable Members opposite. It is not less patriotic to spend your energy in trying to improve the land in which you live, in trying to lighten the toil of the people, and in trying to give them
25 fuller opportunities of life. That is not less patriotic than seeking glory at the cannon's mouth. It is because we are patriots, it is because we love this our country, that we do not wish to see this Bill passed.

> House of Commons Debate, January 1916, on conscription
> – P. Snowden, *Hansard,* 1916.

Questions

a   What position with regard to the war did Snowden adopt?
b   With what argument does he oppose conscription in lines 1–5?
c   To what sinister motives does he ascribe the conscriptionist policies of government members (lines 6–14)?
d   With what definition of his own patriotism does Snowden contrast that patriotism of 'Members opposite' (line 15–19)?
★ e   What was the outcome of the conscription debate in January 1916?

3. Labour and Lloyd George

3rd December (41 Grosvenor Road)

There had been a joint meeting of the Executive of the Labour Party and the Labour M.P.'s to discuss Lloyd George's offer of places in the government – a meeting which came to no decision. Unfortunately the meeting decided to hear Lloyd George, and Henderson
5 arranged that they should meet him immediately (12 o'clock) at the War Office. Thither they went, a private gathering not supposed to be reported. Sidney states that Lloyd George was at his worst, evasive in his statement of policy and cynical in his offer of places in the government. The pro-war Labour members drank in his sweet
10 words, the pacifists maintained a stony silence, whilst Sidney and one or two of the waverers asked questions to which Lloyd George gave non-committal answers. All he definitely promised was a Ministry of Labour and a Food Controller – whilst he clearly intimated compulsory mobilization of labour. The joint meeting
15 discussed these proposals at 8.30 at the House of Commons. The pacifists again laid low – Sidney thought they were playing for the disgracing of the pro-war Labour members by acceptance of Lloyd George's bait of office. The three office-holders in the Asquith administration, together with Barnes and Clynes, all of whom had
20 been against joining Lloyd George, veered round. The miner's members, true to their idiotic rule of never voting without

instructions, expressed no opinion and took no part in the decision. After speeches against taking office, from Sidney, Tyson, Wilson and Walsh, the meeting decided by eighteen votes to twelve in

25 favour of accepting office. There was no display of temper, the most fervent objectors voting silently against it, not really wishing to prevent it. From the narrow standpoint of the pacifist movement, as a sect, the inclusion of pro-war Labour members in the Lloyd George government may be a fortunate circumstance, a

30 discredit to their warlike opinions. Sidney came back glad that he had done his best to prevent a decision disastrous to the Labour Party but inclined to be philosophical. He has long ceased to care about getting his own way and he is always interested, as a student, in watching these breakdowns in Labour democracy.

35 It is very difficult to analyse the state of mind of these men. The prospect of six offices with an aggregate income of some £15,000 a year, to be distributed among eighteen persons, is a big temptation. To enjoy an income of £4,000 a year, or even £1,000, for a year or two, means to any trade union official personal independence for

40 the rest of his life. But I don't believe that this pecuniary motive was dominant in the minds of the eighteen who voted for accepting office. A thorough beating of the Germans may have passed through their minds. But their main motive, at any rate the motive of which they are individually and collectively most conscious, is

45 the illusion that the mere presence of labour men in the government, apart from anything they may do or prevent being done, is in itself a sign of democratic progress. It was this illusion that was responsible for a fanatical fervour with which the I.L.P. started twenty years ago to get labour representatives, whatever their

50 personal character or capacity, on to representative authorities, central or local, from a parish council to the House of Commons. And naturally enough, each individual labour man thinks that he, at any rate, knows his own mind and will get his own way. Neither as individuals nor as a class do labour men realise that they are mere

55 office-mongers when they serve with men of trained intelligence or even with experienced middle-class administrators. It was this illusion that brought Clynes round; he argued that Labour must have some say in the terms of peace. Poor Labour men, they will not get much say in the terms of industrial peace at home, let

60 alone those of the peace of the world!

Beatrice Webb Diaries, entry for 3 December 1916, Norman and Jeanne MacKenzie (eds) *The Diary of Beatrice Webb*, Virago Press, 1984.

Questions

a In what different ways did Labour Party members react to Lloyd George at this meeting (lines 5–25)?

b What did Lloyd George promise Labour in return for their support?

c What devious interpretation did Sidney and Beatrice Webb put on the behaviour of pacifist members at the 8.30 House of Commons meeting (lines 16–30)?

d Why, according to Beatrice Webb, might the majority voting to support Lloyd George have done so (lines 35–60)?

e What role did Labour have in the Lloyd George government formed in early December 1916?

4. MacDonald and Kerensky

My Dear M. Kerensky,

I do not know if you have received the various messages of congratulation which my colleagues and I have sent to you, but I hope you have. You have cheered us in these dark days & restored
5 in our hearts a faith in democracy & a hope that for the first time in history a peace which will be founded on freedom may follow a war. We follow Petrograd events with difficulty because they are recorded by our newspapers coloured & twisted for our own special purposes & the deputation of workmen which our Govern-
10 ment sent will soon be back & will be telling us its own tale which may or may not be reliable. It is of the utmost importance that the Russian Revolution should not be exploited by our government or any other of the Allied governments for their own purposes, but that the Russian people should come into direct contact with our
15 people &, taking council together, should in the common emotions & thoughts of free people announce the programmes upon which Europe may be at peace. I hail with gladness the pronouncements of your Provisional Government. If the wisdom behind these pronouncements & statesmanlike policy embodied in them had
20 guided the Governments of the Allies during the past two years, how different the outlook today would have been. . . .

My own view since the beginning of the war – but I have been in a sad minority which however is steadily increasing in numbers – has been that the chaos now reigning in Europe can be ended only
25 by the people themselves. More emotional pacifism is of no use, a separate peace between Russia and Germany would only leave Europe more helpless than it now is in the hands of evil doers. Russia should therefore put itself with its freshly purified soul & its new enthusiasm for liberty at the head of the European democracy
30 & defining a programme of peace & co-operation with other peoples should offer it to Europe. Then the Governments must make peace upon it or declare to mankind that they reject justice. . . .

We are particularly gratified here with your insistence upon the

35 non-conquest and non-aggression determination of the Russian
democracy. But would it not be possible to carry the matter further
and state at any rate in general outline a programme of peace which
the German democracy, if it be a democracy, could not reject? This
should be drafted after consultation with Allies. I do not think that
40 a consultation with German comrades is necessary in the first
instance because, if drawn up as a document of justice and not of
revenge, it could be issued in the ordinary way to Europe and the
Germans would have to take cognisance of it. . . . I cannot end this
without expressing once more our profound gratitude to your
45 people and our great admiration for them in this crisis of their
national life; and I pray that no evil may divert them from the path
of freedom upon which they have set their feet.

I am, dear M. Kerensky, with fraternal salutations to you and my
comrades of the revolution, yours April 1917
50 J. RAMSAY MACDONALD
Quoted in D. Marquand, *Ramsay MacDonald*, Jonathan
Cape, 1977, pp. 210–11.

Questions

a Who was Kerensky and what had happened in Petrograd (line
7)?
b Why should Kerensky 'have cheered us' (MacDonald and his
colleagues) (line 3)?
c In what senses might the Russian revolution 'be exploited by
our own government' (line 12)?
d What does MacDonald want a newly-democratised Russia to do
(second paragraph)?
e What declared policy of Kerensky 'particularly gratified' (line
34) MacDonald and his colleagues? Why?
★ f What happened to Kerensky and his revolution? Why was it that
MacDonald's high hopes of Russian leadership in European
democracy came to nought?

5. Henderson on Stockholm

The promoters of the Stockholm Conference in Great Britain were
prepared to leave the settlement of the peace conditions to the
Governments, who alone are responsible to the entire nation. But
we of all classes have suffered so much – and which among us at
5 these tables have not got lying beneath the sod a son or someone
else who was near and dear to us? – we belong to the class which
has given most and suffered most, and we shall not allow this
matter to rest in the hands of diplomatists, secret plenipotentiaries,
or politicians of the official stamp, unless they are prepared to have

10　some regard for the opinion of the common people... The
common people, the democracy, did nothing to create the conditions out of which the war came; but the common people have
done everything to realise the ideals for which we entered the war.
　　　I do not withdraw one word of what I have said. I stand by my
15　position. I am not here as an unofficial member of the House of
Commons merely because I supported the Stockholm Conference.
I am here 'in a position of greater freedom and less responsibility'
because I refused to do what I never will do, namely, desert the
people who sent me into the Government.

> Speech by Arthur Henderson, Labour Party Conference,
> Blackpool 1915, quoted by Mary Hamilton, *Arthur Hender-
> son*, Heinemann, 1938.

Questions

a　What was the Stockholm Conference (line 1)?
b　Why was it a matter of such controversy in Britain?
c　For whom (lines 3–13) does Henderson see himself acting?
d　What is the significance of his reference to being 'an unofficial
　　member of the House of Commons' (lines 15–16)?
e　What suspicions does Henderson betray in this passage?

6.　Snowden and Henderson on Peace

Snowden

'I am looking', he said in February 1918, 'for the conclusion of this
war by a union of the democracies of all the belligerent nations.
They have learned that lesson in their common interest, and
although one can hardly say that any good which may result from
5　this war would be anything of compensation for the stupendous
evil which it has created, still it would be something if, as a result of
this war, we had for ever a sweeping-away of the power of those
who have misused their powers in the past, and have used them,
not for the good of the people, but in order to satisfy their own
10　imperialist and selfish aims'.
　　　'All wars are the same', 'You get the same platitudes that "This is
not the time for peace; that you must crush the enemy or you will
have to fight it out again in ten, twenty or thirty years time". The
best, the surest means of having to fight it out again would be to try
15　to pursue the war to a military conclusion. You cannot destroy
militarism by militarism. . . . Suppose the Allies, with the help of
America – I do not believe it possible for a single moment – but
suppose that, with the 10 million men America is going to
transport across the Atlantic, the Allies succeed in inflicting a
20　complete military defeat upon Germany. What is going to be the

effect on the German mind?. . . . It is going to teach them that military power can be a means for effectively serving national aims'.

> P. Snowden, 'February 1918', quoted in Colin Cross, *Philip Snowden*, Barrie & Rockcliff, 1966.

Henderson

In spite of calumny and misrepresentation, we say to our critics: After four years of ruthless slaughter and destruction, in which humanity is slowly bleeding to death, it is time that the military effort was seriously supplemented – not superceded or supplanted,
5 but seriously supplemented – by the pressure of the moral and the political weapon.

As I understand the position of Allied Labour, it is this: We seek a victory, but we do not seek a victory of a militarist or diplomatic nature. We seek a triumph for high principles and noble ideals. We
10 are not influenced by Imperialist ambitions or selfish national interests. We seek a victory, but it must be a victory for international moral and spiritual forces, finding its expression in a peace based upon the inalienable rights of common humanity.

> A. Henderson, Allied Socialist Conference, February, 1918, quoted by Mary Hamilton, *Arthur Henderson*, Heinemann, 1938.

Questions

a How does Snowden hope that the war might be brought to an end (line 2)?
b What greater and more permanent benefit does he hope might accrue (lines 3–10)?
c In what ways was Snowden percipient about future international developments when 'the Allies succeed in inflicting a complete military defeat upon Germany' (lines 19–20)?
d How, according to Henderson, did Allied Labour's position differ from that of the government in the matter of war aims?
★ e To what extent were the warnings heeded, the hopes fulfilled, of Snowden and Henderson during the course of 1918 and 1919?

7. Aftermath to General Election 1919

The Parliamentary revolution in Great Britain has been far more complete. The Liberal Party, which has for years governed the Empire, has been reduced to an insignificant fraction, with all its leaders without exception as the bottom of the poll. The Labour
5 Party has doubled its numbers and polled one-fourth of the entire

voting electorate. It is now 'His Majesty's Opposition', or claims to be in that position. Lloyd George, with his Conservative phalanx, is apparently in complete command of the situation; as the only alternative government there stands the Labour Party, with its completely socialist programme and its utopia of the equalitarian state. But the Parliamentary Labour Party is a very tame lion. All the militants (because they happen to be also pacifists) have been ousted from Parliament. Out of the fifty-nine Labour members twenty-five are miners – for general political purposes dead stuff. Among the others are such fat-heads as Bowerman and such buffoons, simpletons and corrupt persons as Sexton, Thorne and Tillett. The party is led by the respectable but dull-witted Adamson, elected chairman because he is a miner. Clynes and Thomas are the only good speakers and such intellectuals as have survived the election are very inferior.

Sidney reports that at the joint meeting of the Labour Party and the Parliamentary Party it was decided with only one dissentient – O'Grady – to claim the position of His Majesty's Opposition. Whereupon Sidney, in the absence of Henderson (laid up with influenza) offered the services of the Labour Party staff as well as his own to help the Parliamentary Party to carry out its new and difficult duties. The offer was received with friendly appreciation, but no suggestions were made by the M.P.s of how it could be carried out. There is, in fact, some sign that the group of pro-war trade union officials wish to sever their connection with the political organization of the Labour Party and to attempt to run the Parliamentary Party from the offices of the Trades Union Congress.

I have never seen Adamson, the chairman of the Parliamentary Labour Party, before he lunched with us yesterday, except as a squat figure on the platform of the Albert Hall mass meeting just prior to the election. He is a middle-aged Scottish miner, typical British proletarian in body and mind, with an instinctive suspicion of all intellectuals or enthusiasts. . . . He came to us straight from his interview with the Speaker on the all-important question of the claim of the Parliamentary Labour Party to be His Majesty's Opposition.

He repeated slowly and mechanically the Speaker's evasive answer to his claim to be the Leader of His Majesty's Opposition: he was clearly pleased and self-complacent with the vision of himself as the principal figure on the Front Opposition Bench, and only dimly conscious that he would need help to fill the position. He had brought with him a typewritten paper and read from it the requirements which he and his pals among the Labour members had decided were necessary to enable the fifty-eight to tackle Lloyd George and his immense following. 'Two clerks, three typists – we cannot do with less', he deprecatingly insisted. But what exercised

his mind most were the messengers. The Liberals, in the last
Parliament, he said, had had three messengers he thought – and it
55   was clear from his wrinkled forehead and slowly emphatic tone
that he had thought strenuously on this question – he thought that
the Parliamentary Labour Party might take over one of these
messengers to fetch members to important divisions. He waited
anxiously for Sidney's reply. 'There is always the telephone' I said,
60   to relieve the intense gravity of his suggestion, but he shook his
head. No, the messenger was all important. Sidney cheerfully
agreed but gently implied that the Parliamentary Labour Party
would require something more than three clerks, two typists and
one messenger.

> Beatrice Webb Diaries, entry for January 1919, Norman and
> Jeanne MacKenzie (eds) *The Diary of Beatrice Webb*, Virago
> Press, 1984, p. 328.

Questions

a   What, according to Beatrice Webb, were the contrasting fortunes of Liberal and Labour politics in the 1919 Election?

b   Why does she believe the 'Parliamentary Labour Party (to be) a
very tame lion' (line 11)?

c   To what danger, redolent of the 1890s, does Beatrice Webb
point in the behaviour of 'the group of pro-war trade union
officials' (lines 29–30)? Why would this have damaged Labour?

d   What does Beatrice Webb's description of Adamson (lines 34–
64) demonstrate about the leadership and ambition of the
Parliamentary Labour Party in 1919?

e   Why, despite the assemblage of 'dead stuff', 'fat-heads',
buffoons, simpletons and corrupt persons (lines 15–16) which
Beatrice Webb believed characterised the Parliamentary Party,
might the Labour Party derive considerable satisfaction from
the 1919 General Election result?

8. MacDonald and the Peace of Versailles

President Wilson. . . . went to Paris sincerely intending to bring
away from it . . . a League of Nations which would be representative of the people, and would secure peace by removing the causes
of war as they arose. The American, however, was no match for
5   the European diplomatists. . . . M. Clemenceau, the avenger. . . .
has been the supreme power at the Conference. . . . The Italian
Government was frankly out for conquest. . . . Finally, there is Mr
Lloyd George, clear but unanchored, resourceful but without
knowledge. . . . Of all the plenipotentiaries he was the least
10   fitted for his task. He immerses himself in whatever he has in hand;

he is a mere spill on whatever current he happens to float. He has been on both sides of every controversy that has divided the Conference. . . .

Such being the authors, need we be surprised at the proposals? To inflict punishment on Germany, they outrage Europe; millions of Germans, Russians, Jugo-Slavs, Bulgarians, Turks are cut off from their racial kinship; boundaries are drawn without reference to the popular will; areas rich in minerals are attached to foreign states to please the greed of capitalists. . .

The Independent Labour Party and the overwhelming majority of British Socialists may be excused if they behold these events with some complacency. For they all belong to the logic of war. . . . Figs cannot be gathered from thistles. Those who in the name of 'sacred national unity' caught up the emotions which were let loose in August 1914 may reject this treaty, but they sowed the thistles.

> Ramsay MacDonald, *Socialist Review*, July 1919, quoted by D. Marquand, *Ramsay MacDonald*, Jonathan Cape, 1977, pp. 250–1.

Questions

a In what ways did MacDonald believe Wilson to be 'no match for the European diplomatists' (lines 4–5)?

b What are the Versailles proposals (lines 14–19)?

c Why should 'the Independent Labour Party and the overwhelming majority of British Socialists. . . . behold these events with some complacency' (lines 20–2)?

d What does MacDonald mean when he says 'Figs cannot be gathered from thistles' (line 23)?

e How did MacDonald's view of the justice of Versailles subsequently shape his attitude to foreign affairs in the 1920s and 1930s?

9. Labour and Communist

(a) 1919 – an outsider's view

The present unrest in the Army, occasioned by the difficulties of demobilisation, is in grave danger of spreading and of taking the form of an alliance between the soldiers and the extreme section of the workers. There is no natural sympathy or point of agreement between these sections, except that of dissatisfaction, but while the soldiers are only out for understanding and display, a certain section of the workers (whose names and activities are well known to Scotland Yard and the Home Office) are only too ready and eager to fan and foment a passing grievance to inveigle the soldiers

10   unto an alliance with themselves, on the lines of the Soviet Committee. The ultimate end of this manoeuvre would be Revolution and a Soviet form of Government.

    The dangers consequent upon even the slightest success of such a scheme must be patent to anyone who has studied the course of
15   events in Russia. The spread of this spirit is alarming, and evidence can be obtained of a determined effort to emulate the Russian Bolshevik movement of this country. It is also highly significant that while the soldiers are openly declaring their objection to being sent to Russia to fight the Bolsheviki, this very gang of agitators
20   (the ILP) are publishing broadcast a pamphlet 'Hands off Russia', while their press is divided between panegyrics of praise of the Bolshevik form of Government and frenzied abuse of a Government which sends an Army to fight the 'first Socialist Republic'.

> Report by an agent engaged in secret intelligence to Bonar Law, 10 January 1919 (Davidson Papers), quoted by R. K, Middlemas, *The Clydesiders*, Hutchinson, 1965, pp. 88–9.

Questions

a   To what 'difficulties of demobilisation' was the agent referring (line 2)?

b   Why were soldiers 'being sent to Russia to fight the Bolsheviki' (lines 18–19)?

c   What assumptions are made here by the agent about the ultimate aims and ambitions of ILP agitators? How dangerous in your judgement were the activities of these people?

(b) 1921 – an insider's view

The mover of the resolution urged that the affiliation (of the Communist Party) should now be accepted in the interest of unity, but he did not not tell them the kind of unity he was aiming at. If they were going to walk together, they must be agreed; there must
5   be more than unity in name; there must be unity of purpose, unity of principle, unity of conception, and unity of method. No speaker had given a particle of evidence from the Communist Party that they were willing to change their position and to have the kind of unity essential to progress and success. . . . Did the movers of the
10   resolution think that the British Communist Party was going to be allowed by Moscow to adapt their position in order to fit in with this resolution? Any man who sought to persuade himself that that was likely to take place was fooling himself. . . . Moscow had laid down its conditions, and they were inconsistent both with the
15   Labour constitution and the Labour policy. Did anyone seek to persuade the Conference that Moscow stood that day, or ever had stood, for constructive Socialism and real political democracy?

Is that the Party to whom we are to show brotherly love? I happen to be what you call a Methodist, but while we believe in brotherly love, there are occasions on which we believe in repentance, and I want the two to go together. I have not seen any sign of contrition on the part of the Communists as yet.

> Arthur Henderson, Labour Party Conference, December 1921, quoted by Mary Hamilton, *Arthur Henderson*, Heinemann, 1938.

Questions

a What (lines 1–18) were Henderson's objections to the affiliation of the Communist Party to Labour?

★ b How was the issue of communist affiliation to Labour eventually resolved in the 1920s? What was the importance of this decision to Labour's future?

10. Labour Clydesiders' Manifesto

The Labour Members of Parliament for the city of Glasgow and the West of Scotland, inspired by zeal for the welfare of humanity and the prosperity of all peoples and strengthened by the trust reposed in them by their fellow-citizens have resolved to dedicate themselves to the reconciliation and unity of the nations of the world and the development and happiness of the people of these islands.

They record their infinite gratitude to the pioneer minds who have opened up the path for the freedom of the people.

They send to all peoples a message of good–will, and to the sister nations of the British Commonwealth fraternal greetings.

They will not forget those who suffered in the War, and will see that the widows and orphans shall be cherished by the nation.

They will urge without ceasing the need for houses suitable to enshrine the spirit of home.

They will bear in their hearts the sorrows of the aged, the widowed mother, and the poor, that their lives shall not be without comfort.

They will endeavour to purge industry of the curse of unhealthy workshops, restore wages to the level of adequate maintenance, and eradicate the corrupting effects of monopoly and avarice.

They will press for the provision of useful employment or reasonable maintenance.

They will have regard for the weak and those stricken by disease for those who have fallen in the struggle of life and those who are in prison.

To this end they will endeavour to adjust the finances of the nation that the burden of public debt may be relieved and the

maintenance of national administration be borne by those best able
to bear it.

30   In all things they will abjure vanity and self-aggrandizement,
recognising that they are the honoured servants of the people, and
that their only righteous purpose is to promote the welfare of their
fellow-citizens and the well-being of mankind.

> Declaration made by Glasgow's new MPs at a Service of
> Dedication, St Andrews, Glasgow, November 1923, quoted
> by R. K. Middlemas, *The Clydesiders*, Hutchinson, 1965,
> pp. 111–12.

Questions

a What did the Clydesiders here plan to do for society's disadvan-
taged?

b What were the implications of their manifesto for economic
policy?

c In what ways might Philip Snowden and the Labour leadership
take issue with the Clydesiders' prescription for Labour policy?

d How determinedly did the Glasgow MPs subsequently pursue
these manifesto goals?

IV The First Government and Subsequent Trials, 1924–9

The decision to form a government was not straightforward for many Labour leaders exercised by the unique constitutional dilemma posed by the December 1923 election result. Beatrice Webb articulates this, and only reflects a view propagated by Snowden earlier in 1923 – that a minority Labour Government would stand more to lose than to gain by taking office, and that a Liberal–Conservative coalition would be infinitely preferable. But this was to ignore the evidence that the 1923 election had been fought on Protection; that a substantial electoral rejection of Protection had been recorded; and that therefore to permit Baldwin to continue in government after such a result would have been a gross insensitivity to the voter. Furthermore, the idea of Tories' Protection allying with Liberal Free Trade was quite out of the question. In any case MacDonald had few qualms; he saw this as an opportunity to prove that Labour could be trusted. He determined to govern without the partnership of the Liberals and to defy them to throw him out. His ultimate aim was to replace the Liberals on the left of British politics. He assembled a mixed bag of ministers, some refugees from the Liberal Party like Trevelyan and Haldane, and one, a notorious Clydesider left-winger, Wheatley. The character of this and the next Labour Government was shaped by his decision that Philip Snowden be his Chancellor. 'We must imagine', wrote Winston Churchill in *Great Contemporaries*, 'with what joy Mr Snowden was welcomed at the Treasury by the permanent officials. Here was the High Priest entering the Sanctuary. The Treasury mind and the Snowden mind embraced each other with the fervour of two long separated lizards'. As Churchill intimates, Snowden was not to be a radical, free-spending Socialist Chancellor, and this was to lead to tensions, eventually to the Labour split in 1931; many on the left were dismayed at Snowden's accountant's rigidity, his Free Trade Liberalism and Gladstonian obsession with balanced budgets (this 1924 administration was marked by his abolition of McKenna duties, his reduction of food taxes and his determination to use cuts in the naval estimates to lower the National Debt – all orthodox fiscal management which would have been endorsed by W. E. Gladstone).

Domestic initiatives were unimpressive. Wheatley's Housing

Act, which increased the subsidy paid to local authorities to build houses for rent, which led to a great increase in house building, and which went some way to ensuring scarce materials were available for building by Wheatley's diplomacy in drawing interested parties together, was the most notable feature of the Ministry. And even this built on the work of Neville Chamberlain, the Conservative Minister responsible for Housing in 1923. The government had more cause to be pleased with its foreign policy. Here too, it was not without controversy within the party itself. MacDonald, Foreign Secretary as well as Prime Minister, sought to end Franco–German tensions which, in January 1924, manifested themselves in French occupation of the Ruhr. The London Conference he triumphantly managed, which saw the French agree to withdraw from the Ruhr, confirmed French and German acceptance of the Dawes plan, and agreed on new rates of reparations, was criticised from Labour back benchers by such as E. D. Morel and G. Hardie for MacDonald's volte-face since 1918. Certainly the ILP had anathematised Versailles, been hostile to France and had had more than a touch of sympathy for Germany. Yet MacDonald's stroke was timely and ushered in an entirely new phase in European relations for the rest of the 1920s – these might be dubbed the 'Locarno years', the product of lowered tension and increased trust, especially between France and Germany. And at the League of Nations, Arthur Henderson sought to advance the process of disarmament and of collective security by helping devise the Geneva Protocol.

Labour also sought to re-establish links with Russia. The party had to tread very warily; on its left were many who would warmly embrace Bolshevik Russia, the workers' state, but Conservatives, the King himself, the banking and business establishment, all loathed the idea of treating with murderers and appropriators. MacDonald argued that by talking, and reaching an accommodation, with the Russians, something of what had been confiscated could be recovered – the alternative was to do nothing, and regain nothing.

For all the good intentions, and indeed despite the Anglo-Russian Treaty tortuously concluded in the summer of 1924, the Bolshevik issue was to be his Achilles heel. Much of the capitalist press misconstrued the Treaty, painting it as unsecured financial generosity to untrustworthy revolutionaries. The Liberals united with the Conservatives against such loans; then the Campbell case, the proposed government prosecution of J. R. Campbell for seditious writing which appeared to have been dropped after government pressure, brought the Labour administration down. Labour's electoral campaign of October 1924 was dogged by the Communist issue, and the Zinoviev letter sealed the party's defeat. MacDonald too easily accepted Foreign Office advice on the letter's authenticity. Indeed, it has been shown conclusively to have been a White Russian forgery, to which Conservatives and officials who gained access to the document were unwitting parties (see Chester *et al.* below). In the election the Conservatives won 419 seats, Labour 151 and the Liberal Party slid away to 42, spelling the end to its position as a great party challenging for office. Labour had lost 40 seats but paradoxically had increased its vote. MacDonald's strategy of seeking to replace the Liberals as the left alternative to the Conservatives – which had involved doing all that he could to be uncooperative to Lloyd George, Asquith and the Liberal Party – had paid off.

The five years between the first and second Labour Governments were not easy for the Labour leadership. The debate about whether working-class ends were best achieved through democratic, parliamentary gradualism (that is, through Labour's legislative efforts) or through direct action trade unionism (reminiscent of the Syndicalism of 1911 to 1914) was reopened when the miners won Trades Union Congress (TUC) support for a General Strike in 1926. At its end, few Labour people believed that such a General Strike was anything other than a futile gesture. Even Wheatley argued in the 'Eastern Standard' that the General Strike was discredited and self-defeating. However, the Conservatives' revenge in 1927 (the Trade Disputes Act) aroused Labour fury (see Jowett).

From 1925 onwards, elements within the ILP proved increasingly radical; debates over the style and substance of Labour policy were to be the harbingers of the disastrous breakaway by the ILP under Maxton in 1932. The differences are illustrated here, with Maxton and MacDonald arguing over the desirability of Labour embracing red-blooded Socialist nostrums in 1928. MacDonald and the Executive won the battle for bland and generalised intentions which implied faith in the continuing capitalist system. Labour in fact was far less radical in the 1929 General Election than the Liberals whose Keynsian 'Yellow Book' outlined a dynamic policy of regeneration. But the Labour Party did well enough in the campaign to win 288 seats and emerge as the largest party in the Commons for the first time.

1. Cold Feet at the Prospect of Power

On Monday we had a dinner here of leaders – J. R. M., Henderson, Clynes, Thomas and Snowden – to discuss taking office and what exactly they would do if they did. Sidney reports that they have all, except Henderson, 'cold feet' at the thought of office, though all of them believe that J.R.M. ought not to refuse. Henderson wants to take office, to concentrate on unemployment, to set up committees to enquire how the capital levy and national-

isation can best be carried out. Sidney sticks to a bold declaration of policy with the probability of being beaten on the Budget or
10 before. What came out was that Snowden, who thinks he has a right to be Chancellor of the Exchequer, is chicken-hearted and will try to cut down expenditure; He even demurred to a programme of public works for the unemployed. Where was the money to come from? he asked, with a Treasury Clerk's intonation. . . . The
15 leading propagandist socialist like Snowden and even J.R.M. are Utopians who start back from every step towards their Utopia. If Sidney and I were not philosophers we should be disheartened. But what happens to the first Labour Cabinet, acting merely as a stopgap government, is not really of much importance. If they can
20 get over their teething troubles before they have a majority in the House of Commons, J.R.M. may consider himself uncommonly fortunate. And these few weeks or months of office, if it comes off, is like a scouting expedition in the world of administration, a testing of men and measure before they are actually called to
25 assume majority power. . . . .

My general conclusion about the present political situation is this; that while I agree the Labour Party must accept rather than refuse office, it seems absurd, from a mere commonsense community standpoint, that they should govern without having a
30 majority in Parliament or in the country. The honest way out of the impasse, the course which would be approved by the majority of the British people, would be a Liberal-Conservative Coalition – Asquith, Baldwin, Chamberlain, Lloyd George Cabinet, Free Trade and anti-socialist in home affairs and pacific in foreign
35 policy. It is only the struggle for power between the leaders and parties that prevents this carrying out of the clearly expressed will of the people. It is the realization that this Coalition would be the right course that causes a stop in my mind when I look forward to a Labour government, trying to govern in spite of having no
40 mandate for carrying out its distinctive policy. We shall accept because we dare not let it be said that we were not a practicable alternative government.

From Norman and Jeanne MacKenzie (eds) *The Diary of Beatrice Webb*, Virago Press, 1985, pp. 431–2.

Questions

a Who emerges from this description as positive and constructive and who cautious and unambitious?
b What paradox in the behaviour of J.R.M. and Snowden does Beatrice Webb point to in this passage?
c What does Beatrice Webb believe will be the benefit for Labour of 'these few weeks or months of office, if it comes off' (line 22)?

d Explain what Beatrice Webb means when she writes 'it is the realization that this Coalition would be the right course that causes a stop in my mind' (lines 37–8).

2. The London Conference

(a) We are now offering Europe the first really negotiated agreement since the war; every party here represented is morally bound to do its best to carry it out because it is not the result of an ultimatum. This agreement may be regarded as the first
5   Peace Treaty, because we sign it with a feeling that we have turned our backs on the terrible years of war and war mentality.
    Ramsey MacDonald's concluding speech to the London Conference, August 1924, quoted in R. W. Lyman, *The First Labour Government 1924*, (Chapman and Hall, 1957) p. 164.

Questions

a What did MacDonald mean in his boast that 'we are now offering Europe the first really negotiated agreement since the war' (lines 1–2)?
b What did the London Conference do to justify the claim 'that we have turned our backs on the terrible years of war and war mentality' (lines 5–6)?

(b) There is a number of us on these (Labour) Back Benches who are not politicians; that is to say, we are not of this opinion today, and another opinion tomorrow. We have always believed in the policy of no annexations and no indemnities and in
5   working for a peaceful settlement. We still hold to these opinions and if a Vote is taken tonight we shall have the greatest possible pleasure in voting against the government.
    George Hardie, House of Commons speech, July 1924, quoted by R. W. Lyman, *The First Labour Government, 1924*, Chapman and Hall, 1957, p. 162.

Questions

a How does Hardie define 'politicians' (line 2)? What is the thrust of his jibe?
b In what do he and his Back-Bench colleagues continue to believe and why are they disappointed in the London Conference discussions?

3. Labour's Lowered Aspirations

(a) Consequently we shall concentrate, not first of all on the relief of unemployment, but on the restoration of trade. We are not going to diminish industrial capital in order to provide relief. . . . I wish to make it perfectly clear that the government have no intention of drawing off from the normal channels of trade large sums for extemporised measures which can only be palliatives.

> Ramsey MacDonald's speech to Commons 12 February 1925, quoted in R. W. Lyman, *The First Labour Government, 1924*, Chapman and Hall, 1957, p. 135.

(b) Until you have been in office, until you have seen those files warning Cabinet Ministers of the danger of legislation, or that sort of thing, you have not had the experience of trying to carry out what seems to be a simple thing, but which becomes a complex, an exceedingly difficult and laborious and almost heart breaking thing when you come to be a member of a Cabinet in a responsible Government.

> Ramsay MacDonald's speech to the Commons, 28 May 1924, quoted by R. W. Lyman, *The First Labour Government, 1924*, Chapman and Hall, 1957, p. 138.

Questions

a What is MacDonald's strategy for dealing with unemployment? What are his reasons for this strategy?

b How does he characterise the measures back bench proponents of unemployment relief were calling for?

c What is your impression of the impact government and administration had made on MacDonald by the end of May 1924?

4. A Labour Analysis of the Government

The Party in January 1924 could have done one of three things. It could have refused office; that would have been pusillanimous, and the electors would have punished it. ('If they don't want office, they needn't have it' – Lansbury could remember 1912 and foresee that verdict.) It could take office knowing that every bill it produced and every important administrative action, would have to be approved by a Liberal leader who had announced he would not allow anything which had the least taint of Socialism to pass. This had a definite attraction for MacDonald, who felt that in international affairs (he was going to be Foreign Secretary as well as Premier) an enormous advance could be made – a thing that must be to the advantage of the Party. Or, thirdly, it could bring forward a number of genuinely Socialist measures (as Lansbury

would have wished), beginning with the nationalisation of the
15 mines, and when they were rejected, go to the country – not
expecting an immediate victory, but having offered a concrete
programme to the workers and driven false friends and open
enemies together into one camp. One election later the Party might
reasonably hope to return with an independent majority and carry
20 out a balanced Socialist programme.

The second was the policy adopted. The third was for a minute
considered, but Snowden the new Chancellor, recorded that it
was rejected almost instantaneously. Snowden, MacDonald and
Thomas were mainly responsible, as they were for many other
25 decisions in the first and second Labour Governments. It was an
odd triumvirate to have such power – each member thoroughly
disliked the others, and none was of more than second-rate ability.
Yet they were held together by an ultimate unwillingness to make
any fundamental social change and a dislike of their colleagues who
30 tried to push on them the text of the Labour Party's Socialist
programme. As yet, however, they seemed merely affected by an
understandable timidity; Henderson, Clynes, Webb and other
Ministers who were unquestionably loyal to the Party supported
them steadily.

> Raymond Postgate, *Life of George Lansbury*, Longman,
> 1951, pp. 225–6.

Questions

a Which of the three policy options outlined here was adopted?
b Who were responsible for these decisions and what held them
together?
c Why does Postgate believe that this was 'an odd triumvirate to
have such power' (lines 25–6) and how does he rate the three
members himself?
d What was the alternative option which Lansbury would have
wished (lines 13–20)?

5. MacDonald's Assessment of this Party in Government

They have shown the country that they have the capacity to govern
in an equal degree with the other parties in the House. . . . and,
considering their lack of experience. . . . have acquitted themselves
with credit in the House of Commons. The Labour Government
5 have also shown the country that patriotism is not the monopoly of
any single class or party. Finally, they can justly claim that they left
the international situation in a more favourable position than that
which they inherited. They have in fact demonstrated that they, no

10 less than any other party, recognise their duties and responsibilities, and have done much to dispel the fantastic and extravagant belief which at one time found expression that they were nothing but a band of irresponsible revolutionaries intent on wreckage and destruction.

> MacDonald to the King: 10 October 1924, Geo. V K 1958/26, quoted by M. Cowling, *The Impact of Labour, 1920–24*, Cambridge University Press, 1971, p. 359.

Questions

a What three things does MacDonald isolate in the achievements of Labour between January and October 1924?

b What is the importance for MacDonald's Labour strategy of the last five lines in this letter to the king?

c How fair do you think MacDonald's claim to be that they 'have done much to dispel the fantastic and extravagant belief. . . . that they were nothing but a band of irresponsible revolutionaries' (lines 10–13), in the light of your knowledge of the first Labour Government?

6. The Zinoviev Letter

(a) *The Zinoviev Letter*

Executive Committee   Very Secret
  Third Communist International

To the Central Committee
British Communist Party

Presidium
September 15th, 1924
Moscow
Dear Comrades
The time is approaching for the Parliament of England to consider the Treaty concluded between the Governments of Great Britain and S.S.S.R. for the purpose of ratification. The fierce campaign raised by the British bourgeoisie around the question shows that
5   the majority of the same, together with reactionary circles, are against the Treaty for the purpose of breaking off an agreement consolidating the ties between the proletariats of the two countries leading to the restoration of normal relations between England and the S.S.S.R.
10   The proletariat of Great Britain, which pronounced its weighty word when danger threatened a breakoff of the past negotiations, and compelled the Government of MacDonald to conclude the Treaty, must show the greatest possible energy in the further

15 struggle for ratification and against the endeavours of British
capitalists to compel Parliament to annul it.

It is indispensable to stir up the masses of the British proletariat
to bring into movement the army of unemployed proletarians
whose position can be improved only after a loan has been granted
to the S.S.S.R. for the restoration of her economics and when
20 business collaboration between the British and Russian proletariats
has been put in order. It is imperative that the group in the Labour
Party sympathising with the Treaty should bring increased pressure to bear upon the Government and Parliamentary circles in
favour of the ratification of the Treaty.

25 Keep close observation over the leaders of the Labour Party,
because these may easily be found in the leading strings of the
bourgeoisie. Organise a campaign of disclosure of the foreign
policy of MacDonald.

A settlement of relations between the two countries will assist in
30 the revolutionising of the international and British proletariat not
less than a successful rising in any of the working districts of
England, as the establishment of close contact between the British
and Russian proletariat, the exchange of delegations and workers
etc., will make it possible for us to extend and develop the
35 propaganda of ideas of Leninism in England and the Colonies.
Armed warfare must be preceded by a struggle against the inclina-
tions to compromise which are embedded among the majority of
British workmen, against the ideas of evolution and peaceful
extermination of capitalism. Only then will it be possible to count
40 upon complete success of an armed insurrection.

From your last report it is evident that agitation–propaganda
work in the army is weak, in the navy a very little better. It would
be desirable to have cells in all the units of the troops, particularly
among those quartered in the large centres of the country, and also
45 among factories working on munitions and at military store
depots. We request that the most particular attention be paid to
these latter.

The Military Section of the British Communist Party, so far as
we are aware, further suffers from a lack of specialists, the future
50 directors of the British Red Army.

It is time you thought of forming such a group, which together
with the leaders, might be in the event of an outbreak of active
strife, the brain of the military organisation of the party.

Go attentively through the lists of the military 'cells' detailing from
55 them the more energetic and capable men, turn attention to the
more talented military specialists who have for one reason or another
left the Service and hold Socialist views. Attract them into the
ranks of the Communist Party if they desire honestly to serve the
proletariat and desire in the future to direct not the blind mechanical
60 forces in the service of the bourgeoisie, but a national army.

Form a directing operative head of the Military Section.

Do not put this off to a future movement, which may be pregnant with events and catch you unprepared.

Desiring you all success, both in organisation and in your
65 struggle.

With Communist Greetings,

President of the Presidium of I.K.K.I.

ZINOVIEV

Member of the Presidium: McMANUS

Secretary: KUUSINEN

'The Zinoviev Letter', quoted in Chester, Lewis, Fay, Stephen and Young, Hugo, Heinemann, 1967, pp. xi–xiii.

Questions

a How true had it already been that a group in the Labour Party had assisted in the shaping of the Anglo-Russian treaty which now awaited ratification (lines 21–4)?

b How does the letter foresee the Treaty assisting revolutionary affairs?

c What are comrades exhorted to do in the last third of the letter?

(b) MacDonald explains

On the 21st the draft – the trial draft – was sent to me at Abervavon. . . . I did not receive it until the 23rd. On the morning of the 24th I looked at the draft. I altered it, and sent it back in an altered form, expecting it to come back to me again with proofs of
5 authenticity, but that night it was published (Cries of 'Shame').

I make no complaints. . . . The Foreign Office and every official in it know my views about propaganda. . . . On account of my known determination to stand firm by agreements and to treat them as Holy Writ when my signature has been attached to them, they
10 assumed that they were carrying out my wishes in taking immediate steps to publish the whole affair. They honestly believed that the document was authentic, and upon that belief they acted.

If they acted too precipitately, what is the accusation against us? Why don't these newspapers say we are in too great haste? Ah, that
15 won't catch votes against us. . . . Therefore, they have to put up the story that we shilly-shally. . . . Only nine days have elapsed from the first registering of the letter and the publication of the dispatch last Friday (Cheers). . . .

But that is not the whole story. . . . It came to my knowledge on
20 Saturday that a certain London morning newspaper. . . . had a copy of this Zinovieff letter and was going to spring it upon us. . . .

. . . .(H)ow did it come to have a copy of that letter?. . . . I am also informed that the Conservative Headquarters had been spread-

ing abroad for some days that. . . . a mine was going to be sprung
25 under our feet, and that the name of Zinovieff was to be associated
with mine. Another Guy Fawkes (laughter) – a new Gunpowder
Plot. . . .

   (T)he letter might have originated anywhere. The staff of the
Foreign Office up to the end of the week thought it was authentic.
30   . . . I have not seen the evidence yet. All I say is this, that it is a
most suspicious circumstance that a certain newspaper and the
headquarters of the Conservative Association seem to have had
copies of it at the same time as the Foreign Office, and if that is true
how can I. . . . avoid the suspicion – I will not say the conclusion –
35   that the whole thing is a political plot? (Loud cheers). . . .

> Ramsay MacDonald, Cardiff, 27 October, quoted by D.
> Marquand, *Ramsay MacDonald*, Jonathan Cape, 1977,
> pp. 385–6.

Questions

a Summarise MacDonald's explanation of his handling of the
   Zinoviev letter.
b What circumstances led him, he claims, into considering that
   the whole thing is 'a political plot' (line 35).

(c) The conspiracy unmasked

The Zinoviev letter, with its chilling exhortation to British Communists to gird themselves for the revolution, effectively destroyed
the electoral chances of Britain's First Government when it went to
the polls in October 1924. It also eclipsed any prospect of the
5   Anglo-Russian trade treaties being ratified by the British Parliament. Both consummations were devoutly wished by all the
conspirators who had made the letter's publication possible. It was,
most of all, a triumph for the tiny group of white Russian émigrés
who had originally penned this particular example of Bolshevik
10   extremism over the forged signature of Grigory Zinoviev, the
Russian president of the Third International.

   But their efforts alone could never have achieved success. To
bring the exercise to fruition, the co-operation of other parties was
needed – parties who had to be bluffed into believing that the letter
15   was genuine before they could throw their weight behind the
enterprise. These were the phase-two conspirators, men who,
having once convinced themselves of the letter's authenticity, with
only the most exiguous evidence, were prepared to employ the
most elaborate and sometimes highly dubious devices to ensure
20   its publication. Into this category fell an oddly assorted bunch;
the British intelligence service, Conservative Central Office, the
Foreign Office and the *Daily Mail*. Each group of conspirators had

its own methods, and at times they worked in almost complete ignorance of what the others were doing – so much so that even
25 after the event none of those involved could be sure who deserved most credit for engineering this most unscrupulous, and potent, election 'gimmick' in British political history.

> From the Prologue to *The Zinoviev Letter* by Chester, Lewis, Fay, Stephen and Young, Hugo, Heinemann, 1967, p. xv.

Questions

a For whom was the Zinoviev letter a 'triumph'?
b Which other parties co-operated 'to bring the exercise to fruition' (line 13)?
c What were the two major consequences of the letter?

7. Labour and the General Strike

4th May (Passfield Corner)

When all is said and done we personally are against the use of the General Strike in order to compel the employers of a particular industry to yield to the men's demands, however well justified these claims may be. Such methods cannot be tolerated by any
5 government – even a Labour government would have to take up the challenge. A General Strike aims at coercing the whole community and is only successful if it does so and in so far as it does so. Further, if it succeeeded in coercing the community it would mean that a militant minority were starving the majority into submission
10 to their will and would be the end of democracy, industrial as well as political. Sooner or later – in Great Britain, sooner rather than later – the community as a whole would organize to prevent such coercion by penal legislation. But there arise emergencies when it is better to fight even if you cannot win than to take oppression lying
15 down. And this is especially so when the struggle is within a good natured community who will recognise that men who fight and lose must be generously treated by the victorious party: that a willingness to fight, with the certainty that you will lose, implies a big grievance. Whether these considerations hold good on this
20 occasion I do not know. To us it was as clear as noonday that with the trade union movement in its present state of mind this weapon of a final strike would be used. When it has been tried and failed, as fail it will, the workers will be in a better frame of mind for steady and sensible political action. . . .
25   The net impression left on my mind is that the General Strike will turn out not to be a revolution of any sort or kind but a batch of compulsory Bank Holidays without any opportunities for

recreation and a lot of dreary walking to and fro. When the million
or so strikers have spent their money they will drift back to work
and no one will be any the better and many will be a great deal
poorer and everybody will be cross. It is a monstrous irrelevance in
the sphere of social reform. If it be prolonged a week or ten days it
may lead to reactionary legislation against trade unionism and
possibly to a general election. But I doubt it. If the government
keeps its head and goes persistently and skilfully to work in
reconstructing services the General Strike will peter out; and the
noxious futility of this mild edition of the 'dictatorship of the
proletariat' will be apparent to everyone, not least to trade unionists
who find their funds exhausted and many of their most able
members victimized by being permanently displaced by patriotic
blacklegs! There will be, not only an excuse but a justification of
victimization on a considerable scale. . . .

For the British trade union movement I see a day of terrible
disillusionment. The failure of the General Strike of 1926 will be
one of the most significant landmarks in the history of the British
working class.

Future historians will, I think, regard it as the death gasp of that
pernicious doctrine of 'workers' control' of public affairs through
the trade unions, and by the method of direct action. This absurd
doctrine was introduced into British working-class life by Tom
Mann and the Guild Socialists and preached insistently before the
war, by the *Daily Herald* under George Lansbury.

> From Norman and Jeanne MacKenzie (eds) *The Diary of
> Beatrice Webb*, Virago Press, 1987, pp. 76–7.

Questions

a On what grounds are the Webbs 'personally against the use of a
   General Strike' (lines 1–2)?
b What does Beatrice Webb anticipate the outcome of the strike to
   be?
c What relevance does she see this strike to have for working-class
   progress?
d How does she believe the strike will be judged in the future?
★ e How much in touch with main line Labour thinking on the
   strike do you think Beatrice Webb might have been?

8. Jowett Castigates the Tory Backlash, 1928

Parliament has been used to the fullest extent possible to punish the
workers. . . . The Trades Disputes Act was the first fruit of the
defeat of the miners. Having got the miners down and incapable at
the moment of resistance and knowing, as Mr Baldwin did, that

5   the fighting funds of the Trades Unions were just then depleted,
     the attack on the Unions and their political funds was launched
     immediately and pressed to the utmost limit in severity.
        Having struck at the Trades Unions through the Trades Disputes
     Act, the next step in the capitalist offensive against the working
10   class was to cut off supplies to the unemployed and make sure of a
     reserve supply of impoverished work-seekers who would be forced
     by threatened starvation to accept low wages.
        First, grants for relief works were reduced almost to nothing.
     Then the conditions limiting payment of unemployment benefit
15   were made more severe. Single men and unemployed workers with
     relatives who are not also destitute were ruled out altogether from
     receipt of extended unemployment benefit. Tests of willingness to
     work which cannot be complied with by large numbers of unem-
     ployed workers were imposed.
20   Whereupon, the conditions applying to payment of Poor Law
     relief were also tightened, lest there should be found in this last
     resort some slackening in the competition for jobs by unemployed
     workers.
        Where duly elected Guardians in poverty stricken areas have
25   refused to starve the workless poor, they have been removed from
     office and replaced by paid agents of the capitalist Government
     who are willing to do the dirty work.

                    F. Jowett, Bradford Trades and Labour Council Year Book
                    1928, quoted by Fenner Brockway, *Socialism over 60 years*,
                    George Allen & Unwin Ltd, 1946.

Questions

a   In what ways did the Trades Disputes Act punish the workers?
    What were the Tory government's intentions in pushing
    through this Act?
b   How does Jowett convey the unfairness of this assault on the
    Unions?
c   Explain 'the next step in the capitalist offensive against the
    working class', (lines 9–10) in your own words.
d   How far do you think the Conservaties *were* guilty of pushing
    through a co-ordinated programme 'to punish the workers'
    (line 2)?
e   Does Jowett at any time in this account reveal his own personal
    feelings about Government policy?

9.   The Cook–Maxton Manifesto, 1928

To the Workers of Britain

For some time a number of us have been seriously disturbed as to
where the British Labour Movement is being led. We believe that

its basic principles are: (1) An unceasing war against Capitalism. (2) That only by their own efforts can the workers obtain the fullest product of their labour.

These basic principles provided the inspiration and the organization on which the party was built. They were the principles of Hardie and the other pioneers who made the Party. But in recent times there has been a serious departure from the principles and policy which animated the founders. We are now being asked to believe that the party is no longer a working-class party, but a party representing all sections of the community. As Socialists we feel we cannot represent the views of Capitalism. Capitalism and Socialism can have nothing in common.

As a result of the new conception that Socialism and Capitalism should sink their differences, much of the energy which should be expended in fighting Capitalism is now expended in crushing everybody who dares to remain true to the ideals of the Movement. We are convinced that this change is responsible for destroying the fighting spirit of the party, and we now come out openly to challenge it. We can no longer stand by and see 30 years of devoted work destroyed in making peace with Capitalism and compromises with the political philosophy of our Capitalist opponents.

In furtherance of our effort, we propose to combine in carrying through a series of conferences and meetings in various parts of the country. At these conferences the rank-and-file will be given the opportunity to state whether they accept the new outlook, or whether they wish to remain true to the spirit and the ideals which animated the early pioneers.

Conditions have not changed. Wealth and luxury still flaunt themselves in the face of the poverty-stricken workers who produce them. We ask you to join in the fight against the system which makes these conditions possible.

Yours fraternally,
A. J. COOK
JAMES MAXTON

From McAllister, *James Maxton Portrait of a Rebel*, John Murray, 1935, p. 187.

Questions

a Who was A. J. Cook?
b How do the authors differ from Labour Party leaders in their attitudes to capitalism?
c What do they believe was happening to 'everybody who dares to remain true to the ideals of the Movement' (line 18)? Who is opposing these fundamentalists?
d How do they propose to counter this opposition?
e How was the Cook-Maxton manifesto treated within the Labour movement?

V The Bankers' Ramp – The Second Labour Government, 1929–31

Labour returned to power in June 1929 as the largest party in the Commons, but the Liberals still held the balance; their 59 seats when added to the Conservatives 261 could bring down the Labour Party (which had won 287). MacDonald's second Cabinet was as conservative as his first with Snowden an immovable force again as Chancellor. Henderson, a critic of MacDonald, went to the Foreign Office, Thomas was placed in charge of unemployment policy, Clynes became Home Secretary, and the most adventurous appointments were reserved for the minor posts, notably in the elevation of Oswald Mosley to the Chancellorship of the Duchy of Lancaster, Hugh Dalton to the position of Parliamentary Secretary to the Foreign Office, George Lansbury, the pacifist and architect of Poplarism, to the post of First Commissioner of Works, and Herbert Morrison to the Ministry of Transport.

The minority nature of the administration once again profoundly influenced the character of the Labour government. It is clear that the legislative programme was circumscribed by the Liberals' desire to flex their parliamentary muscles – usually without wishing to deliver a knock-out blow which might precipitate an unwelcome General Election. The Liberals demanded some return for their continued support of Labour in office and electoral reform was conceded by MacDonald to Lloyd George in 1931, although the bill which would have ended the first-past-the-post system perished with the government in August 1931. They also champed at the bit over the seeming impotence of Labour to tackle the immense task of curbing unemployment. And, at various points in the two years, Labour ministers believed that their last hours in government had come, only to find that the Liberals had reprieved them; the Coal Mines Bill late in 1929 was a notable example of this brinkmanship. It all militated against long-term, bold planning of policy.

There were some domestic successes for the government. The Coal Mines Bill progressed to the statute book in 1930 and hours worked by miners were reduced from eight to seven and a half hours revoking the Tory legislation of 1926. However, a reorganisation commission to introduce rationalisation of production and of mines (something on which Snowden was very keen, to increase Britain's export potential) was stillborn.

At the Ministry of Transport, Herbert Morrison set out the policy (later enacted by the National Government) for London Transport, gathering up the capital's buses and underground trains as part of the responsibility of a new public corporation, and anticipating the Morrisonian nationalisation of Attlee's government. Arthur Greenwood at the Ministry of Health revived the languishing Wheatley reforms for housing and initiated slum clearance, and Christopher Addison, Minister of Agriculture, negotiated successfully with free trade interests to push through the Agricultural Marketing Act in 1931, permitting boards of producers to fix prices and to market their produce. Yet all this did not amount to much given the severity, and apparent intractability, of the economic crisis which befell the country from October 1929.

Abroad, Labour added to its reputation for constructive peace-making won in 1924. MacDonald was the first British Prime Minister to visit the United States while in office – in 1929 – and there he did much to pave the way for a three-power naval treaty (with Japan) which was signed in London in April 1930 and which provided a 'holiday' in battleship construction to 1935, limited submarine building and warfare, and which stipulated the size of navies for the three powers. The treaty, according to MacDonald, 'proved how, when the world likes, the menace of arms can be removed by treaties regulating their development'. Indeed, it exemplified Labour's conviction that international agreement, collective security and phased disarmament could make the world safe from future war. Henderson as Foreign Secretary worked hard to realise the ideal; he tried to bring Soviet Russia back into the fold, not perturbed by the disasters in this sensitive area suffered by Labour in 1924. So, the Labour Government resumed diplomatic relations with Soviet Russia in October 1929 – and the questions of a British loan to Russia, and of the pre-revolutionary debt owed by the Russians, were quietly dropped. At the League of Nations Henderson emerged as the dominant figure because he was trusted by French and German alike; he won that respect by working successfully for the early withdrawal of allied troops from the Rhineland, by committing Britain to the Optional Clause by which disputes would be submitted to the jurisdiction of the Court of the League of Nations at the Hague, and by pushing tirelessly to give effect to the League's commitment to setting up a Disarmament Conference. This was eventually set up in February 1932 and before the Labour Government had collapsed he had been accorded the singular honour of being chosen its President. Yet even as he worked to extend the League's influence, its insufficiency in the face of the cynical and determined was being revealed by the Japanese in Manchuria.

Overshadowing and dwarfing these Labour achievements was the frightening spectre of unemployment. In January 1930, after a six-month trade revival which accompanied Labour's return to office, 1,533,000 men were out of work; by March the figure had risen to 1.73 million and by December 1930 it had soared to 2.72m. It was to approach three million by the time that Labour sundered in August 1931. It was an international problem associated with the collapse of Wall Street in October 1929 which directly affected American investment in Europe and indirectly led to the collapse of world commodity prices, and so to a declining demand for manufactured goods. The Labour party was torn apart – literally – by the consequent unemployment. Many party members fervently believed in the evils of capitalism and saw this crisis as proof of the system's imminent collapse. A few on the Left welcomed the opportunity to hasten its end, but were unclear about what to do to replace it. Strangely, many in the party and in the trade union movement espoused an old Liberal economic philosophy of adherence to gold and to free trade, which they held with almost religious fervour, and this made it impossible for them to react imaginatively to the unprecedented situation. Oswald Mosley and a few in his intimate circle dared to press the case for a radical solution based on government borrowing to invest in public works and so to stimulate the economy. His dramatic and unavailing clash with J. H. Thomas and with Philip Snowden – High Priest of financial rectitude and of the balanced budget – is a key moment in inter-war politics. A Keynsian solution was rejected, a brilliant young Labour minister was lost, and a British Fascist party was born.

The crisis increased in its severity in 1931. The demise of the Labour Government that summer has caused continuing controversy, many in the Labour movement excoriating MacDonald for his decision to form a National Government. He has been portrayed as a vain, ambitious man, sacrificing party and friends to hold on to power and being far too easily gulled by international bankers in the process. For his part, he has argued that his Cabinet and the Trades Union Congress (TUC) – all recognising the impossibility of abandoning the gold standard (for hyperinflation was thought to be the inevitable alternative) and the need to achieve a balanced budget to win the American Bank credits which would halt the run on gold – fought shy of facing the logic of their position. He, and Snowden, thought that cuts to balance a budget, badly out of kilter through the heavy drain of unemployment benefit payments, had to be made (in line with the suggestions of the May Committee Report of summer 1931) to avoid the greater catastrophe of the economy's complete collapse; his critics believed that the unemployed had suffered enough by the very nature of their unemployment and that for Labour people to cut their benefit was tantamount to treason. In the crucial Cabinet meeting of 23 August 1931, the impossibility of Labour's position was clearly

evidenced; the barest majority (11:9) voted for cuts in unemployment payments (and cuts in teacher and forces pay) but those in the
minority like Henderson were determined to resign on the issue.
Henderson wanted Labour to stay united, and the party to resign in
favour of a Conservative-Liberal administration. MacDonald believed this to be a feeble shirking of responsibility; and so found the
appeal of the King not to desert the country, to be patriotic, and to
do his duty, attractive. Whether one believes MacDonald to have
deserted his party for the embrace of the establishment and the
bankers, or to have been doing his self-appointed duty extremely
reluctantly, the effect was the same; to split Labour spectacularly
and with extremely damaging electoral consequences for the remainder of the 1930s.

1.   End of Year Gloom

1929 has been an historic year. Ruth's election to Parliament, the
General Election and 6½ months at the Foreign Office.

How long shall we last? After the shake-up on the Coal Bill one
feels pretty insecure but, though we might go out at any time, it is
5   possible that we might yet last two years. Stamfordham told
Canon D. that the King wasn't going far from London in the New
Year for fear of an early general election. What would happen at an
election? Have we become markedly unpopular yet? I think not,
but even a loss of 20 or 30 seats (net) would upset the Parliamentary
10   position pretty fatally. Issues, however, rise and fall, and we may
do well in the New Year. Unemployment will fall at least
seasonally, for a month or two, and some of our Bills should be
popular – Housing and Slum Clearance and the Budget, for
instance – and should also afford a basis for Lab-Lib co-operation in
15   the House.

The Labour Government as a whole is already pretty disappointing with bright patches. Uncle's star has been very much in the
ascendant, both in the Party and in the House and George Lansbury
is trying to brighten people's lives and let in more sunlight, and
20   Morrison is very competent, and Johnston very persistent and
Greenwood is first rate [Uncle – the nickname commonly applied
to Arthur Henderson]. But Trevelyan is terribly disappointing.
This is a bitter discovery after our good political comradeship. But
he is almost incredibly stupid and is said always to put his case
25   badly in Cabinet and can't even see that he ought to carry his
Higher School Leaving Age Bill this session, so as to get it safely
passed, while there is yet time, and make the L.E.A.s (Local
Education Authorities) realise the need to get schemes ready for
1931. The effects on unemployment which will, I believe, be very
30   striking, can't in any case come till the autumn of 1931. And this

may be too late for us. And pensioning off the old is hung up too. Damn!

Thomas and Maggie Bondfield are the two most obvious failures of the Government. Few have anything good to say of either of them. MacDonald has been messing about again with the idea of the Economic General Staff, and having economists to lunch. But nothing concrete comes of it.

The back benchers are weak, as I have just said, on practical ginger – except on unemployment insurance. But this may improve, as some of the new recruits grow more experienced.

As to Foreign Policy, I am not so unhappy though my hopes of any big achievement on naval disarmament are rather dim. But Uncle has asked for 27th January for the Optional Clause in the House, and we should make another good show at Geneva, if we live so long, next September. The Russians, however, will be very troublesome – the new Communist Party daily in London is quoting stuff from the Third International already! But they aren't really urgent, especially the Chinese.

India – thank goodness! – isn't our pigeon. The recent proceedings of the National Congress, with their outcry for independence, are not exactly comfortable. But, if the Simon Commission produces a good report, and we act on it quickly, things may brighten up. 'Storm over India' is a dramatic caption, and some say the Government will fall over India. But I doubt this.

> Hugh Dalton in B. Pimlott (ed.) *The Political Diary of Hugh Dalton*, Jonathan Cape, 1986, pp. 85–6.

Questions

a To what does Dalton refer when he talks of 'the shake-up on the Coal Bill' (lines 3–4)?

b Which of Dalton's predictions for the coming year were to prove to be misplaced?

c Why was it that 'Uncle's star has been very much in the ascendant, both in the Party and in the House' (lines 17–18)?

d On what grounds does Dalton criticise Trevelyan? What was to happen to Trevelyan during his second Labour administration?

e For what were Thomas and 'Maggie' Bondfield responsible? Why would Dalton have described them as 'the two most obvious failures of the Government' (lines 33–4)?

★ f How did MacDonald's idea of the Economic General Staff evolve during the life of the Government? What is its significance?

★ g How did the Government subsequently fare over India?

2. Henderson Explains his Foreign Policy

I have been criticised by some of those who do not think with us for signing the Optional Clause at all. Others have attempted to ridicule us, by contending that our signature was stultified by the attachment of too many reservations – by the exclusion, that is, of
5   too many classes of dispute from our acceptance of the Court's jurisdiction.

They cannot have it both ways; they cannot both be right. What have we, in fact excluded? In the first place, we have excluded disputes arising prior to the ratification of our signature of the
10 Clause. That is surely a right and proper reservation. To make our ratification retrospective might lead to incalculable complications, by encouraging the resuscitation of matters long since disposed of. Next, we excluded disputes in respect of which the two parties may agree to have recourse to some other method of peaceful settlement
15 – a wholly reasonable and unexceptionable reservation. Further, we excluded disputes between different members of the British Commonwealth of Nations and those which fall by international law exclusively within domestic jurisdiction. If anyone contends that either of these classes of dispute is suitable for reference to an
20 international tribunal, I beg most respectfully to differ from him. Our only other reservation was one which had the effect of suspending proceedings in the Court if either of the parties prefers to refer the matter to the Council of the League. Failing settlement by the Council, or agreement between the parties for further
25 suspension, the dispute reverts automatically, after twelve months, to the Court. In that way can that reservation be held to weaken our signature? It is entirely in harmony with the spirit and the letter of the Covenant, and does not invalidate our acceptance of the Court's jurisdiction, failing other methods of peaceful settlement.
30 There remains the class of dispute which is not amenable to settlement by these means, and which, failing settlement by the Council, may possibly lead to war. This is a matter which is receiving our earnest consideration.

We are looking for more substantial all-round reduction of
35 armaments than anything hitherto contemplated. Nothing less than a new kind of national security – security not for one nation at the price of danger to its neighbours but common security for all nations, whether great or small. Through the League of Nations, by our policy of disarmament, we mean to carry it.
40 I had made it known at an early stage that British public opinion was insistent upon the withdrawal of British troops from the Rhineland and that we felt that the time had come for an early complete evacuation of German occupied territory. French public opinion differed from British public opinion in this, and M.
45 Briand's task was thus far more difficult than mine. But M. Briand

and Dr Stresemann have worked together so often before that I never doubted that an agreement would be reached. They both showed that clear misunderstanding of each other's problems and that good will that count for everything in international relations.
50   The result was complete agreement upon the political issue. Our troops numbering 6,192 began to move on September 14th and over a thousand of them are already home. The evacuation of the British forces will be completed by December 14th. The Belgians hope to have their troops removed by the middle of December
55   and the French complete the evacuation of the second zone in December and the third in June. By that period there will not be a single soldier in any of the occupied parts of German territory.

> Speech by Henderson at Brighton Labour Party Conference, October 1929, quoted by Mary Hamilton, *Arthur Henderson*, Heinemann, 1938, pp. 332–4.

Questions

a   Explain the reference to the 'Optional Clause' (line 2). What reservations does Henderson say he has made and why?
b   What remaining ambition has Henderson got for the League?
c   What concrete step does Henderson boast he has already taken for the disarming of Europe?

3.   Oswald Mosley's Unorthodox Views

It is absolutely necessary that the whole initiative and drive should rest in the hands of the Government themselves. . . . After all, it was done in the War; there were revolutions in the machinery of government one after another, until the machine was devised. . . .
5   by which the job could be done. . . . It is to the Home Market that we must look for the solution of our difficulties. (Hon. Members: Hear, hear!). . . . We have to get away from the belief that the only criterion of British prosperity is how many goods we can send abroad for foreigners to consume. . . . How is money for public
10   works to be raised, out of revenue or out of loan? £100,000,000 out of revenue! Who will suggest it in the present situation? It is 2s on the Income Tax. It must be raised by loan. If the principle of a big loan is turned down then this kind of work must come to an end. Given, however, a financial policy of stabilisation, that Treasury
15   point of view cannot hold water. It would mean that every single new enterprise is going to put as many men out of employment as it will employ. . . . If it is true it means that nothing can ever be done by the Government or by Parliament. It means that no Government has any function or any purpose; it is a policy of
20   complete surrender. Why is it so right and proper that capital

should go overseas to equip factories to compete against us, to build roads and railways in the Argentine or in Timbuctoo, to provide employment for people in those countries while it is supposed to shake the whole basis of our financial strength if anyone dares suggest the raising of money by the Government of this country to provide employment for the people of this country? This nation has to be mobilised and rallied for a tremendous effort, and who can do that except the Government of the day? If that effort is not made we may soon come to crisis, to a real crisis. I do not fear that so much, for this reason, that in a crisis this nation is always at its best. This people knows how to handle a crisis, it cools their heads and steels their nerves. What I fear much more than a sudden crisis is a long, slow, crumbling through the years until we sink to the level of a Spain, a gradual paralysis, beneath which all the vigour and energy of this country will succumb. That is a far more dangerous thing, and far more likely to happen unless some effort is made. If the effort is made how relatively easily can disaster be averted. You have in this country resources, skilled craftsmen among the workers, design and technique among the technicians, unknown and unequalled in any other country in the world. What a fantastic assumption it is that a nation which within the life-time of every one has put forth efforts of energy and vigour unequalled in the history of the world, should succumb before an economic situation such as the present. If the situation is to be overcome, if the great powers of this country are to be rallied and mobilised for a great national effort, then the Government and Parliament must give a lead. I beg the Government tonight to give the vital forces of this country the chance that they await. I beg Parliament to give that lead.

> From a speech in the Commons, May 1930, quoted by R. Skidelsky, *Oswald Mosley*, Macmillan, 1975, pp. 214–16.

Questions

a   In what ways did Mosley's demand for active Government 'initiative and drive' (line 1) challenge orthodox opinion in 1930?

b   How did Mosley's economic policy proposals differ from the policy pursued by the Labour Chancellor of the Exchequer?

★ c   What aspects of Mosley's speech might be said to anticipate his later political development?

4. Oswald Mosley's 'Amazing Blunder'

22nd May; Committee Room 14 packed out (with Labour Party people) at 8 p.m. Lord Oswald (Dalton's nickname for Oswald Mosley) gives a long harangue which rather impresses the meeting.

A parade of loyalty and no personalities. 'Not a general vote of
censure on Government, but only a vote of censure on its
unemployment policy'. This doesn't help very much. A great
parade of statistics. Long term reorganisation. Imports Board.
Loans for work-retiring pensioners. Raising school leaving age. All
these last three to cost the Budget only £10m a year and retiring
pensions of £1 a week, plus 10/- for wife at sixty to cost only
£2m a year. (Fantastic jugglery!). . . . Present inequity between
depressed and prosperous areas. (This passage much applauded.)
Ends with a typical Mosley peroration about saving Government
and Party, and millions whom we represent. Considerable applause
at the end. At one point, not quite sure of himself, refers to himself
as 'a newcomer and outsider'. Then MacDonald. Not at all
convincing or effective. Then Hayday (a Trade Unionist), critical
of Lord Oswald. What would be thought in the Trade Union
world of an Executive member who resigns and then tries to turn
membership against Executive. Then he moves an amendment,
encouraging the Government's policy, its executive and administrative record, reaffirming that unemployment is inseparable from
capitalism, recognising that the present depression is partly due
to world causes, but urging a more vigorous policy. Bromley
supports Lord Oswald in a speech of garrulous egotism. Rhys
Davies throws doubt on efficiency of offer of retiring pension of £1
a week at sixty. Thomas, half hysterical, speaks of 'we who built
up the movement on the soap box. . . . and took a job that I
knew would shatter my reputation. . . . I have always been loyal
to my colleagues. . . . I have always played in the team. . . . the
greatest moment of humiliation in my life'.

Uncle (Henderson) at 10.30 rises to wind up. A difficult atmos-
phere, not very friendly to the Government. . . . Congratulates
all on high level of discussion. Critical moment in history of
Party. Bouquets for Lord Oswald. He also has had to face
resignation. Not true that principle of retiring pensions has been
abandoned. It couldn't be. We fought last election on it. If it were
to be suggested that this Government would never, at any time or
in any form, bring in such a scheme, there would be at least one
more resignation. (Mild sensation.) A vote tonight would be
disastrous whatever its results. Appeal to Lord Oswald to withdraw both resolution and amendment. Then a further discussion on
unemployment can follow at another Party Meeting. Situation has
changed. P.M. has been released from heavy work of Naval
Conference. He is now taking charge of unemployment discussion.
Let us not give any comfort to our enemies. Let us do the big
thing. He is the oldest Labour Member here. Twenty seven years
ago he entered the house. He has never made an appeal in all this
time more earnestly, or more conscious that he is right, than
tonight.

Lord Oswald rises. He wishes to make a few observations. He noticed that Uncle said retiring pension scheme was not abandoned. But Snowden in his Report of Cabinet Sub-Committee
55 had said that 'the Government should repudiate this scheme, and grandiose loan plans'. Snowden who had sat silent all the evening snaps 'That's not true'. Lord Oswald says, 'Then will you tell us what you did say?' 'No', snaps Snowden. Lord Oswald very ruffled, then says that he has been appealed to by senior member(s?)
60 of the Party to withdraw. He thinks a decision now would be more courageous than postponement. But he is seeking an accommodation and he will be willing to postpone a decision till after further discussion, and to move that discussion be adjourned. Uncle jumps up and says this is not what he meant. We must decide tonight.
65 Lord Oswald says, if this is so, he must ask for a decision on his resolution tonight. An amazing blunder! He had the ball at his feet. He might have left the meeting a hero, the darling of the back-benchers, a moral victor. But his last words provoke a growl of surprise and indignation. One can feel votes turning away from
70 him. There are shouts for a straight vote. On a vote Moseley gets 29 votes against 210. It is a crushing defeat.

The Left has sat all night, drilled and silent. Lord Oswald has so safeguarded himself, after much preparation clearly, from their direct embrace.
75 And so we go forth at 10.45 with a passage thronged with waiting pressmen. Lord Oswald is the worst tactician of the age! 'Whom the Gods wish to destroy. . . .' A head swollen to the size of an elephant.

> Hugh Dalton, in B. Pimlott (ed.) *The Political Diary of Hugh Dalton*, Jonathan Cape, 1986, pp. 112–14.

Questions

a   How, according to Dalton, did Mosley try to appear conciliatory, even when presenting his alternative unemployment policy?
b   What line did Hayday, the trade unionist take? Why might this be surprising?
c   What does Thomas's speech (lines 27–31) illustrate about his policies, his political values and his state of mind?
d   What role did Henderson play in this Party meeting? What was the gist of his appeal to the meeting?
e   What was Oswald Mosley's 'amazing blunder'? What is Dalton's opinion of Mosley from this passage?

5.   A Modern Perspective on Mosley and Labour

In this at least he was right. The Labour Party was not the sort of party Mosley imagined it to be. Ideologically it was; psychologically it was not. The Labour Party's dream-world was particularly luxuriant in utopias. However, its dreams were the fantasies of the impotent. It was terrified of either acquiring or using power. And without power there could be no utopia, not even the first halting step on the way. To cover up the fear there was an attractive rationalisation; Labour Government lacked a majority. But as Élie Halévy remarked, not unfairly, after the 1931 débâcle: 'I tell you frankly that I shudder at the thought of the Labour Party ever having a real majority, not for the sake of capitalism but for the sake of socialism'. This fear of power was rooted in the psychology of the underdog. Although they dreamed of being on top, the working class were in fact on the bottom: and the whole of their struggle was directed not towards the acquiring of power for which inwardly they felt themselves unfitted but towards limiting the power of those who had it.

The Labour Party existed not to govern but to attack government, whether it be government in industry, or government in Parliament. Power was for others – Tories, Landlords, employers. What Labour wanted was to tear down the mighty from their seats and exalt the humble and meek. Hence arises the paradox that in the inter-war years the party of state power was the least willing of all to use state power. While Lloyd George Liberals and young Tories preached the philosophy of state intervention, the Labour Party practised the philosophy of small government. From this irony was born in Mosley's mind the idea for a new type of movement which combined the passion for social reform with the *übermensch* psychology that could alone bring it about.

R. Skidelsky, *Oswald Mosley*, Macmillan, 1975, p. 206.

Questions

a   Why does Skidelsky believe that Labour was not, psychologically, 'the sort of party Moseley imagined it to be' (lines 1–2).
b   Explain the paradox that Halévy articulates in lines 9–12 and that Skidelsky expresses when he argues 'that in the inter-war years the party of state power was the least willing of all to use state power' (lines 22–4).

6. G. D. H. Cole Recalls Labour's Dilemma in 1930

From the first, the Labour Government was between the two fires over its handling of the unemployment problem. On the one hand it had to face the criticisms of its own left wing, which regarded unemployment as a by-product of capitalism, incurable within the capitalist system, and demanded a frontal attack on capitalism, either in the form of extensive socialisation of industry or in the I.L.P. form of bankrupting capitalist industries by insistence on a Living Wage, and then taking over every section that defaulted on this obligation; and on the other hand it was continually pressed by the Liberals, who believed that the problem could be solved under capitalism by a combination of reformed credit and banking policy, public control and stimulation of investment, and public works on a scale which Snowden, who would have had to raise the money, regarded as prohibitively expensive. In facing these critics the Government had to take account of the gold standard, to which Churchill had brought Great Britain back in 1925, and of the fact that Snowden believed fanatically in the gold standard and would sanction nothing that might endanger its maintenance. With the gold standard in force, any fall in world prices or demand meant reducing the prices of British exports in terms of pounds, shillings and pence; and this meant not only that wages could not be raised, but also pressure to reduce them steadily as the world situation got worse. Moreover, as long as Great Britain adhered to Free Trade and put practically no restriction on imports, every contraction in world demand set other industrial countries competing more keenly in the British home market as well as in other export markets, and involved an attempt to dump surplus goods in Great Britain, at the same time as other countries were putting additional restrictions on their imports either by raising tariffs or by direct or financial controls. Snowden, however, believed as fanatically in Free Trade as in the gold standard and would agree to nothing that would interfere with either.

In these circumstances, it was utterly impossible to check the rise in unemployment, which followed partly on export dumping in the British home and export markets and partly on the necessity of internal deflation in order to maintain the rates of exchange in face of falling world prices. Either going off the gold standard or a drastic policy of restrictions on imports might have made some contribution to dealing with the problem, though neither could have prevented Great Britain from feeling some of the effects of the developing world crisis. When Snowden would have no truck with either expedient, there was no alternative left to allowing unemployment to go on rising until the arrival of the inevitable financial crisis that would force the country to act in sheer self-preservation.

Why, it may be asked, was the situation not dealt with by over-riding, and if necessary replacing, Philip Snowden? The answer is, first, that Snowden held a very strong position in the Party as its one recognised financial expert, as well as on the strength of his reputation for Socialist inflexibility. Neither Mac-Donald nor most of the other members of the Cabinet had any understanding of finance, or even thought they had. Graham, who had and saw the problem, was too weak to stand up to Snowden.

Thomas wanted a tariff, which was anathema to most of the Labour Party as well as to the Liberals, but had no grasp of the
55 financial problem. Henderson was too busy on foreign affairs to pay much attention to economic problems, and was, in any case, never consulted by MacDonald about such matters. The Economic Advisory Council, of which I was a member, discussed the situation again and again; and some of us, including Keynes, tried
60 to get MacDonald to understand the sheer necessity of adopting some definite policy for stopping the rot. Snowden was inflexible; and MacDonald could not make up his mind, with the consequence that Great Britain drifted steadily towards a disaster of whose imminence the main body of Labour M.P.s and of the Labour
65 movement were wholly unaware. All these troubles came to a head only in 1931; but they were there in 1930, plain to be seen by those who were prepared to look facts in the face.

> From G. D. H. Cole, *History of the Labour Party since 1914*, Allen & Unwin, 1948, pp. 235–7.

Questions

a Explain in your own words the 'two fires' (line 1) between which the Labour Government was caught in 1930.
b What was the 'Living Wage' (line 8)? Explain the thinking behind it.
c Why was unemployment rising, according to Cole? What radical policies might have alleviated the problem?
d Why were radical policies not implemented?
e What are Cole's views of MacDonald and Snowden? Why should care be taken in assessing the validity of his views?

7. A Left-Wing Reaction to the Crisis of February 1931

The plain fact is that the banks ever since the war ended have had control of Governments.

The banks are responsible for the policy which has increased the value of war loan pounds from 155 to somewhere near 255,
5 whereas the French cancelled four-fifths of their war debt by giving their tenpenny francs the value of twopence.

It is the banks that are pushing the Government into the suicidal policy of increasing production without at the same time increasing the purchasing power of the working class. Or, to put the matter in
10 another way, without redistributing the national income so as to consume the additional amount of goods produced. How on earth can the capital for greater production of consumable goods result in anything else than gluts and growing unemployment, if the

working class, which includes nine-tenths of the nation, have their
15 purchasing power decreased instead of being correspondingly
increased?

Sooner or later the banks will have to be faithfully dealt with.
Why not deal faithfully with them now, when the need is so great
and everybody who thinks sees it?
20 Why should the present generation of workers be denied decent
houses, adequate pensions for the aged, the sightless and the infirm,
schools and plenty of food for their children, to pay off small
chunks of war debt and to keep a parasitic creditor class in luxury
on the remainder?. . . . Prohibit foreign investments as you did in
25 war-time or tax them so heartily that they will repent.

> F. Jowett, *Bradford Pioneer*, 20 February 1931, quoted in
> Fenner Brockway, *60 years of Socialism*, George Allen &
> Unwin, 1946, p. 287.

Questions

a By whom does Jowett believe government policy to be
influenced?
b What does Jowett argue is essential to avoid 'gluts and growing
unemployment' (line 13)?
c Why were workers being forced to sacrifice the basic elements
of a decent life? In what ways did his reaction challenge
Snowden's orthodoxy?

8. Different Contemporary Views on the August 1931 Crisis

A. Criticism of the government's handling of the May Committee Report

It was an act of incredible folly, as I felt when I first knew of it, to
allow the May Report to be published without any comment or
declaration of policy. The impression was at once conveyed to the
foreigner that we had a deficit of £120,000,000 which could not be
5 cured except by knocking off £60,000,000 from unemployment
pay, which he knew we should not do and that the Government
had no policy. It ought to have been delayed until balanced
statement and a definite policy could be published simultaneously.

> Survey for 1931 by the Royal Institute for International
> Affairs, quoted in Mary Hamilton, *Arthur Henderson* Heine-
> mann, 1938, p. 372.

B. Snowden's account

During the succeeding three days, that is from the Thursday,

August 20th to Sunday August 23rd, Mr MacDonald and I, with the consent of the Cabinet, had frequent interviews with the leaders of the Opposition. They maintained their attitude that, if the Government could not go beyond the figure of £56,250,000 as the total of their economies, they would feel compelled to call for an early meeting of the House of Commons when they would unite and defeat the Government. Faced with this probability, the Cabinet turned its attention to seeing whether any more could be done. I ought to add that the Opposition leaders were wholly dissatisfied with the proposals of the Cabinet for reducing the cost of the unemployment payments. The Cabinet, therefore, turned its attention to seeing what could be done to meet the demands of the Opposition leaders in this matter. There was, as I have said, an almost equal division of opinion in the Cabinet on the question of a reduction in the unemployment benefits. It was therefore decided that Mr. MacDonald and myself should be empowered to submit, tentatively, to the Opposition leaders a suggestion that, if we could increase the economies by £20m – namely, £12,500,000 from the Unemployment Grants and £7,500,000 from other sources – they would regard that as satisfactory. We were placed in a difficult position in making this suggestion, because we had no assurance that, if it were accepted by the Opposition leaders, the Cabinet would agree to it. However, we put the proposal before them, and we received the impression that, if this could be done, they would regard the total of our economies as satisfactory. But they urged that the bankers should be consulted, and, if they were satisfied, the Opposition leaders would raise no further objection.

> From Philip Snowden, *An Autobiography*, Nicolson & Watson, 1934, p. 944.

C. *Mary Hamilton remembers Labour's agonies*

In the endless discussions of the Cabinet, first this possibility and then that was explored. There was no one who was not prepared to make some yield of personal predilection and even of personal conviction, if the national financial situation could be saved. Later recriminations were to darken counsel, and make it impossible for representatives of different views of what it was right to do to respect each other. But, at this stage, there is no need to deny either to those who refused to accept cuts, or to those who thought that, morally, and in a higher interest, they had got to accept them, the sincerity of their sense of differing duty. Henderson, on this issue, was not one of those who wavered. His opposition to, and refusal of, unemployment cuts was unvarying. But he was torn and tortured by a conflict of loyalties of a most poignant kind. In August, 15 years ago, he had been torn by a similar, though far less acute conflict. Then, in the midst of a great war, he had been rent

between loyalty to a government of which he was a member, but whose policy he thought was going wrong, and a Party with whose policy he agreed on a major international issue. But, in 1917, his associates in the Cabinet had been strangers: to-day they were
20 friends, associates in a whole lifetime's common work. No harder choice could be presented to any honest man. When that man is almost one of affectionate heart and tenacious personal fidelity, the choice has a cruelly cutting edge. Henderson took his problem away with him to the quiet of the country. He had a cottage near
25 Lancing; there during the Sunday, he wrestled with himself, alone. When he came back from the fateful Cabinet meeting in the evening he knew his course. Principles came before persons. How often he had said that from the platform! He had said it, and he meant it; he was going to act upon it now. The policy of the
30 Opposition should be carried out, by the Opposition. A Labour Government might die, but the Labour Party must live.

> Mary Hamilton, *Arthur Henderson*, Heinemann, 1938, p. 382.

Questions

a On what grounds does the anonymous author of the Royal Institute Survey (Extract A) criticise the government? What were the details of the 'May Report' (line 2)?

b What impression does Snowden convey in Extract B of the Labour government's relations with the Opposition?

c Against what government package did the Opposition leaders suggest they would raise no objection? (Extract B).

d Why was it considered important 'that the bankers should be consulted' (Extract B, line 27)?

e What (Extract C) was Henderson's position on the Cabinet's policy of August 1931? What 'conflict of loyalties' (line 13) did he face?

9.   The End of the Government

A.   *MacDonald explains to his colleagues*

My dear Shinwell,
I need not say how deeply I regret the necessity for the resignation of the government, but I wish to thank you most sincerely for the assistance you have given and the pleasure I have had in working
5 with you. It is a very painful decision that has had to be taken, and I wish you to have no doubt at all about what it was. We were on the verge of a financial crisis which if not dealt with within the space of

days, would have meant not cuts of 10 per cent or anything of that
kind, in unemployment pay, but would have disorganized the
whole of our financial system, with the most dire results to the
mass of the working class. It may take a little time for people to
understand what are the issues and the alternatives to what I have
done with some colleagues, but the events of to-day have shown
that, but for the step which has been taken, before this week had
well begun we should have been in the midst of a crushing
calamity. The government that has been formed is not a Coalition
but a co-operation between individuals who are banded together to
avoid the disaster. No parties are involved in it, and as soon as the
country gets on an even keel again, the Government will cease to
exist.

While the trouble lasted no other question could overshadow it,
and no action which did not directly meet it, and which took time
in coming into operation, was of the least use. We should have been
fiddling beautiful music whilst Rome was burning. We had to
follow what we considered to be a line necessary for the maintenance – even if in a temporarily limited form – of everything we
stand for. I know it is hard to understand this, but I am certain that
its truth will be seen as the days go on when the Party will have to
stand impotently by whilst its work is being undone by others.
Having failed to meet the immediate situation we should have been
swept away in ignominy before the end of this week by popular
clamour, so that it can be proved later on, whatever offence we
have caused at this moment, we have created the conditions under
which the Party can continue as an Opposition and allow the
public, saved from panic, to consider a return of our general policy
when things have become more normal.

I am,
Yours very sincerely,
J. Ramsay MacDonald

A letter of 24 August 1931, quoted by E. Shinwell in *Conflict
without Malice*, Odhams Press, 1955, pp. 110–11.

B. Beatrice Webb's view

24th August: 6.30 p.m. (Passfield Corner)

The Fall of the Labour Government, 1929–31. Just heard over the
wireless what I wished to hear, that the Cabinet as a whole has
resigned, J.R.M. accepting office as Prime Minister in order to
form a National Emergency Government including Tories and
Liberals; it being also stated that Snowden, Thomas and alas!
Sankey will take office under him. I regret Sankey, but I am glad
the other three will disappear from the Labour world; they were
rotten stuff, each one of them for different reasons. A startling

10 sensation it will be for those faithful followers throughout the
    country who were unaware of J.R.M.'s and Snowden's gradual
    conversion to the outlook of the city and London society. Thomas
    has never been a socialist and will probably cease, like other
    ci-devant trade union leaders, to be even formally on the side of the
15 Labour movement. So ends, ingloriously, the Labour Cabinet of
    1929–31. A victory for the American and British financiers – a
    dangerous one, because it is an open declaration, without any
    disguise, of capitalist dictatorship, and a brutal defiance of the
    Labour movement. The Third International will gloat over the
20 'treachery' of MacDonald, Snowden and Thomas. . . .

25th August (Passfield Corner)

    Sidney came back early in the afternoon of our second Fabian
    Garden Party. He was exhausted, and rather upset by the queer end
    of the Labour Cabinet – but delighted to be out of it all. At the
25 seven o'clock Sunday night Cabinet meeting, J.R.M. brought back
    an inconclusive answer from the U.S.A. and British financiers to
    the revised Cabinet scheme of economies, indicating that more cuts
    in the insurance benefit would be required to satisfy the U.S.A.
    financiers. Whereupon nine members of the Cabinet, headed by
30 Henderson, revolted and stated that they would not go so far in
    cutting the dole even as J.R.M. had done on their behalf. Where-
    upon the Prime Minister left for Buckingham Palace and adjourned
    the Cabinet for twelve o'clock on Monday. At that meeting he
    announced he had accepted a commission to form a National
35 government. His colleagues listened with the usual English compo-
    sure, Henderson intimating that discussion would be out of place;
    after which the meeting proceeded to wind up the formal business
    about documents etc.; passed unanimously a vote of thanks to the
    P.M., proposed by Sankey, and without further leave-taking left
40 the Cabinet room. Whereupon Sidney joined up with Henderson
    and Lansbury and some six others, and went off to lunch at the
    Office of Works to discuss the situation. There was a certain relief
    that their association with MacDonald was at an end, and a very
    distinct opinion that he had meant to come out as Premier of a
45 'National' government all through those latter days of panic and
    confusion.
        Whether MacDonald had already arranged with Snowden and
    Thomas some days ago no one knew, but it is assumed so. What is
    in doubt is whether MacDonald himself, and the Conservatives and
50 Liberals with whom he negotiated, expected a considerable group
    of Labour members to follow him. If he or they did, they will be
    grievously disappointed.
        One of the good results of the National government under Mac
    is that it unites, as no other event could, the whole of the Labour

55   movement under Henderson in determined opposition to the
policy of making the working class pay for the mistakes of the
financiers. . . .

> Norman and Jeanne MacKenzie (eds) *The Diary of Beatrice
> Webb*, Virago Press, 1987, pp. 254–7.

Questions

Extract A

a What evidence for MacDonald's motives in taking (this) 'very
painful decision' (line 5) is there in this letter to Shinwell?

b How did MacDonald explain away the fact that his decision was
splitting the Labour party?

c What does MacDonald believe will be the immediate future for
the Labour party?

Extract B

d What is Beatrice Webb's opinion of the motives of MacDonald,
and the other Labour ministers who joined the new National
Government?

e How does she explain the fall of this Labour Government?

f What silver lining is she able to find for Labour in this formation
of a National Emergency Government?

Both Extracts

g Evaluate the case for and against MacDonald in his decision
to tender the Cabinet's resignation and form new National
Government.

VI   The Wilderness – Labour, 1931–40

The demise of the Labour Government in August, 1931 split the party. Shock amongst those Labour politicians who stayed outside Ramsay MacDonald's new National Government soon turned to bitterness at the perceived betrayal, a bitterness directed at the four Labour members of the Cabinet, MacDonald himself, Sankey, Thomas and Snowden. MacDonald had initially talked of a Cabinet of individuals formed for only temporary ends, to preserve the country's gold standard and international confidence. The collapse of that confidence after the Invergordon mutiny in September 1931, the subsequent flight from gold (which, contrary to received wisdom, was not followed by rampaging inflation), and the calling of a General Election in October for a 'Doctor's Mandate' to deal with the economic crisis for the government, completed the Labour party's disillusionment with MacDonald and his fellow disloyalists. In the General Election Labour slumped to 46 seats, the great majority of her parliamentary leaders lost their seats, and Lansbury and Attlee led the party through the following traumatic years.

The party subsequently made a strong and steady electoral recovery. Before the next election it won ten by-elections, notably the East Fulham by-election in 1933 which seemed to be a victory for pacificism, was probably more a protest against the Means Test, and certainly succeeded in frightening Baldwin, who said 'It was a nightmare', largely because it conjured up the spectre of spectacular Labour gains at the next General Election. These vivid imaginings were not to materialise in October 1935, but Labour did gain over 100 seats, winning 154 in total, still a long way behind the National Government's 431 seats, but as far as popular vote was concerned agreeably improving on the 1929 poll at 37 per cent. The National Government's majority, however, remained largely un-impressionable, and was not dented until May 1940.

Labour's electoral recovery was achieved against a background of continuing internal party strife. After a brief radicalism, the leadership of the party settled down to an orthodox and conserva-tive position, emphasising the desirability of discipline, unity and electability. The Left, a heterogeneous collection of groups, did not agree. It interpreted 1931 as an Establishment conspiracy whereby monarchy, Conservative Party, bankers and Fleet Street had conspired to dish socialism. The Independent Labour Party (ILP) wanted Labour to abandon compromise and commit itself to full-blooded implementation of a socialist programme as the only solution to a crisis which represented the death-throes of the capitalist system. The intemperancy of such as Maxton in 1932 carried the ILP into disaffiliation from the Labour party and ended a long, sometimes fruitful and sometimes fraught relationship which had survived throughout the party's youthful history. This did not end the activities of the Left; left-wing members who did not follow the ILP into oblivion formed the Socialist League to articulate their views. Stafford Cripps was a driving force. The capitalist conspiracy continued to exercise him and his followers, and they believed in the absolute necessity of a future Labour Government passing an Emergency Powers Act within hours of taking office to ensure a decisive pre-emptive socialist strike before capitalism retaliated. Many in the Socialist League were profoundly suspicious of the whole parliamentary democratic process, seeing it as a means of gathering socialists into that aristocratic embrace which effectively smothered radical action. Some indeed drifted on into Communism. And it was natural that the Socialist League should look in 1937 to unity (with communists and the ILP) to try and stimulate effective support for the Spanish Republicans locked in a Civil War it seemed they would lose. For its pains the Socialist League was dissolved. Some on the Left like Aneurin Bevan did not join the Socialist League, but they were still forcible critics of the Labour leadership's apparent timidity in failing to support enthusiastically the Hunger Marchers or in compromising Labour Party foreign policy in 1935 (see below).

Yet the Left was not responsible for laying down the socialist foundations on which the next Labour Government would build the New Jerusalem. Its suspicions of Parliament blinded it to the possibility that genuine reform could be carried there. Its distaste for Mosley after his performance in 1931 led it to reject Keynes because Mosley had espoused his views. So it was the right and moderate sections of the party which formulated through the 1930s the policies which would be enacted in 1945. Men like Douglas Jay, Hugh Gaitskell and Dr Hugh Dalton – intellectuals, dons, economists – absorbed and refined Keynes's lessons and determined to implement them. Nor was this the only realignment in Labour's thinking. Just as the conversion to Keynsian economics reversed the policies of MacDonald and Snowden when leaders, so the enthusiasm for nationalisation in the 1930s overturned the suspicions with which they had greeted ILP nationalisation policies in 1928. For 'Socialism and Peace' in 1934 and 'Labour's Immediate Programme' in 1937, spelt out policies for stimulating employment and for nationalising the commanding heights of the economy. They also elucidated Labour's view of a planned economy, of increasing attraction to Attlee, propagated by Morrison and involving the creation of a National Investment Board to direct the development of industry in the country. By 1939 the programme, which was carried through in 1945, was – in many areas – fleshed out.

The most divisive issue of all within the party was that of foreign policy. At first, and while the International Disarmament Conference survived, it was not so, and Labour could unite around a policy of collective security and disarmament. Slowly the views of the leadership, the Executive and the powerful trade union bosses evolved; the changing international situation showed that collective security could only be achieved with military under-pinning. When, after the Italian invasion of Abyssinia, it became clear that the League of Nations had failed to keep the peace, there was an acceptance amongst these Labour people of the need to rearm to fight Fascism. Perhaps the 1935 Labour Conference was the critical moment in this acceptance. By the time of Munich it was, paradoxically, Attlee who expressed revulsion at Chamberlain's tame surrender; and early in September 1939 it was Greenwood, the Deputy Leader of the Labour Party, who was exhorted to 'speak for England' in a House of Commons outraged at the evasions of the government.

The Left had a more tortuous passage in resolving its foreign policy position in the 1930s. Bevan and Cripps, amongst others, called either for out-and-out pacifism or at least for an attack on rearmament, arguing that the Establishment must not be afforded the military means to turn on domestic workers. Spain changed this; the fight of the underdog, the Republic, to resist Franco's army inspired many on the Left to fight. It led Left leaders to castigate the government for its non-intervention (which permitted the Nazis and Italian Fascists a free run in helping Franco), and to call for arms to fight Fascism. The failure of its campaign led first to the alignment of the Left under the banner of a United Front in 1937. In 1938, with Chamberlain's 'sacrifice' of Czechoslovakia and evident lack of enthusiasm for alliance with Soviet Russia to halt Hitler, Cripps issued a call for a Popular Front, an alignment (so it was hoped) of Liberals, moderate Conservatives, communists and Labour. The leadership rejected the call, suspicious of any connection with communists and, after 1931, equally suspicious of any collaboration with non-socialists. Cripps and Bevan were expelled from the party for the persistence with which they pursued the unacceptable.

When the war came, the Labour Party – anti-Fascist and convinced of the mission cause this time – rallied to the government. However, the inadequacies and failures of the succeeding eight months convinced Attlee and others of the need for the removal of Chamberlain and it was the Labour Party Conference decision in Bournemouth to withdraw support from Chamberlain and offer it to either Halifax or Churchill which brought about the Prime Ministership of Winston Churchill in May 1940.

1. Beatrice Webb on MacDonald and Snowden's Tergiversations

23rd September 1931 (Passfield Corner)

When, on the Sunday afternoon, two ex-Cabinet Ministers and two ex-Under-Secretaries were discussing the probable character of the P.M's summons to Henderson to return to London, not one of them had the remotest inkling that the decision was 'to go off the
5 gold standard'. The silly old Snowden had broadcast the day after the formation of the National government the horrors – the bankruptcy of all business, and death by starvation of the working class – implied by the 'loss of the pound'; no suggestion of giving up parity had been even mooted at any Cabinet meetings. The
10 saving of the parity of the pound had been the very purpose of the negotiations with U.S.A. and France, the reason for ousting the Labour government and forming the National government. At the meeting with the T.U.C. Thomas and Mac had slobbered over the agony of 'going off gold', had vividly described the sudden and
15 simultaneous disappearance of all luxuries and most necessities from the homes of the workers. And now, having dismissed the Labour government and exacted the 'economy' Budget and thrown the unemployed back on to the Poor Law, the bankers advise the government to repudiate gold and go back to the prosperous
20 pre-parity days of 1918–26. The plaudits of the Press on Monday and poor Snowden's second broadcast explaining that the whole difference between disaster and a 'new start for industry' lay in the fact that 'the Budget had been balanced' – a 'scrap of paper' which the Labour Cabinet was quite willing to provide – was a comic and
25 humiliating exposure of the consummate trickery of the financial world, when it feels itself menaced either in profits or power. It is also, alas, not a very complimentary sidelight on the financial acumen of the Labour Cabinet and not one of them saw through the little conspiracy of the City. And at the cost to taxpayers of
30 some £10 millions by the way of the fruitless loan.

From Norman and Jeanne MacKenzie (eds) *The Diary of Beatrice Webb*, Virago Press, 1987, p. 259.

Questions

a How does Beatrice Webb convey her distaste for the Labour politicians who joined the National Government?

b Why was it that 'not one of them [the ex-Ministers] had the remotest inkling that the decision was "to go off the gold standard" ' (lines 3–5)?

c How does Beatrice Webb justify the assertion that this decision 'to go off the gold standard' was the result of the government's trickery of the financial world (lines 25–6), a 'little conspiracy of the City' (line 29)?

d What is her view, therefore, of the policy and the politics of the last days of the Labour Cabinet, a month before she wrote this diary entry?

2. Snowden's bitterness spills over

However anxious we may be to advance the social services, we cannot do it when the resources from which the cost must come are drying up. A nation, like an individual, cannot go on increasing expenditure when income is falling, unless it wants to be landed in
5 bankruptcy. It became clear to me in the early part of this year that we were on the edge of national bankruptcy, and drastic measures would have to be taken if that catastrophe were to be averted. . . .

I mention the fact now because no harm is likely to be done since we have balanced the Budget, but the situation was so serious that
10 by the middle of November, if we had allowed things to drift, there would have been no money to pay the unemployment benefit. What we have done has saved the unemployed from that plight. . . .

I would warn the electors against being influenced by considera-
15 tions other than the one issue. That one issue on which you should vote is, as I have stated elsewhere, whether we should have a strong and stable Government in this time of national crisis, or whether we should hand over the destinies of the nation to men whose conduct in a grave emergency has shown them to be unfitted to be
20 trusted with responsibility. . . .

I hope you have read the election programme of the Labour Party. It is the most fantastic and impracticable document ever put before the electors. All the derelict industries are to be taken over by the State and the taxpayer is to shoulder the losses. The banks
25 and financial houses are to be placed under the national ownership and control, which means, I suppose, that they are to be run by a joint committee of the Labour Party and the Trade Union Council. Your investments are to be ordered by some board, and your foreign investments are to be mobilised to finance this madcap policy.
30 This is not Socialism. It is Bolshevism run mad. I have been an advocate of sane and evolutionary Socialism for forty years, but I have always attacked such a revolutionary policy as is set out in this manifesto. . . .

At the time when national entrenchment is vital, when above all
35 else confidence in our sanity is needed, this programme is issued – a
programme which, were it taken seriously, would destroy every
vestige of confidence and plunge the country into irretrievable
ruin. . . .

I am supporting this National Government as a temporary
40 expedient to do the work which I would fain have seen a united
Labour Government undertake. I am doing this because I do not
want to see the work of a lifetime brought to rack and ruin.

To none more than the working classes is it more vital that a
strong National Government should be returned. I ask them to
45 believe that I give them this advice under a profound conviction
that in doing so I am still serving the best interests of the working
classes and safeguarding their future progress.

Good night.

> From an election broadcast by Philip Snowden, 17 October
> 1931, quoted by Colin Cross, *Philip Snowden*, Barrie &
> Rockcliff, 1966, pp. 318–9.

Questions

a What benefits does Snowden claim to have flowed from his
economics policy of the previous year (lines 1–13)? What is 'the
one issue' (line 15) from which Snowden warned the electors
not to be deflected?

b What 'revolutionary policy as is set out in this manifesto' (lines
32–3) does Snowden attack in this broadcast?

c Describe Snowden's attitude to the party of which until a short
time previously he had been a member.

d How might Snowden justify the claim in lines 46–7 that 'I am
still serving the best interests of the working class and safeguarding their future progress'?

3. The Labour Party Manifesto, October 1931

A decisive opportunity is given to the nation to reconstruct the
foundations of its life.

The Capitalist system has broken down even in those countries
where its authority was thought to be most secure.
5 It fails to give employment to many millions of willing workers.
It accumulates vast stocks of commodities which it is unable to
distribute.

To re-establish its position, it now demands from the unemployed and the wage-earner the surrender of their hard-won
10 standard of life; and it seeks to force the Government of this
country to restrict or abandon those social services which the

Labour Party believes to be an essential condition of a democratic society.

False Front of 'Unity'

15 The Labour Government was sacrificed to the clamour of Bankers and Financiers. Because it placed the needs of the workers before the demands of the rich, a so-called 'National' Government was installed in its place to wrest from Parliament the authority to satisfy them.

20 The policy of that Government has proved a disastrous failure. Formed to maintain the gold standard which it declared in panic-stricken accent to be the indispensable condition of national safety. Within less than three weeks it abandoned that standard with the insolent explanation that industry would benefit by the

25 change.

Having failed completely in its original object, it now seeks from the electorate a mandate for the impossible task of rebuilding Capitalism. Composed of men who differ profoundly on all the main principles of public policy, unable to agree upon any of the

30 essential methods by which to restore prosperity to the nation, this ill-assorted association of life-long antagonists seeks a blank cheque from the people for purposes it is unable to define. Acutely divided within itself; headed by men who are now acting in direct contradiction to their own previous convictions; certain, in the near

35 future, to split into fragments, it makes the shameless pretence of being the instrument of national unity.

The Labour Party is confident that the country will not be deceived by claims so arrogant and so dishonest.

We must plan or perish

40 The Labour Party seeks a majority from the electorate upon the basis of a coherent and definite programme.

It reaffirms its conviction that Socialism provides the only solution for the evils resulting from unregulated competition and the domination of vested interests. It presses for the extension of

45 publicly-owned industries and services operated solely in the interests of the people. It works for the substitution of co-ordinated planning for the anarchy of individualistic enterprise. Labour insists that we must plan our civilisation or perish.

> Quoted in F. Bealey, *The Social and Political Thought of the British Labour Party*, Weidenfeld & Nicolson, 1970, pp. 129–30.

a What assumption is made about the Capitalist system in the opening 13 lines? What proof is adduced to support this contention?

b How does the Manifesto justify the claim that 'the policy of the Government has proved a disastrous failure' (line 20)?

c Explain the phrase 'this ill-assorted association of life-long antagonists' (lines 30–1). How correct was the prediction 'certain, in the near future, to split into fragments' (lines 34–5) about the fate of the National Government?

d What are the elements of Labour's 'coherent and definite programme' (line 41)? In what way does the programme differ from the policies pursued by the second Labour Government?

4. Private Doubts about Labour's Direction

I saw Uncle Arthur yesterday. I do not think he is very well, though he says he is. I found him a bit upset with the sort of forward policy we aim at. He talked of miners and others demanding something to go on with, and not being content to wait for
5 Socialism; this seemed like our old friend Gradualism with a vengeance. I reminded him that at Scarborough [the Labour Party Conference there had adopted a programme Lansbury might well have written himself] all our speakers deliberately and after due consideration declared we could not deliver the goods re-Social
10 services etc. within the capitalist system. I also said that what mattered was that the programme we fight on shall be a Socialist one, full blooded and unmistakable; but he seemed to doubt, even if he had a majority, the wisdom of punching our policy right home. I tried hard to make him see that if we had a majority we
15 could not be turned out, and told him I am certain the bankers and financiers will endeavour to sabotage us and whether we like it or not we should be forced to deal with the Banking system. . . .

But my final thought is that A. H. is terribly worried about the
20 party, that he feels Labour is in the wilderness for a long period unless we can trim our sails so as to catch the wind of disgust which will blow Mac and his friends out and that he is not anxious for us to be too definite about Socialist measures as our first objectives. Put them in our programme but be sure when we come to power
25 we keep on the line of least resistance. He is not dishonest or to be blamed for this attitude; like me he has spent his whole life doing small things while advocating his 'changes'. You must make him

see the movement he has done so much to foster will perish if once
again it gets lost in the morass of opportunism.

> From a letter from George Lansbury to Stafford Cripps,
> undated (probably end of 1931), quoted by Raymond Post-
> gate, *The Life of George Lansbury*, Longmans, 1951, pp. 279–
> 80 (A. H. are the initials of Arthur Henderson).

Questions

a What is the difference between Henderson and Lansbury over
Labour Party policy as outlined in the first paragraph of
Lansbury's letter here?

b What does Lansbury mean by 'this seemed like our old friend
Gradualism with a vengeance' (lines 5–6)?

c With what justification could A. H. (Henderson) hope in 1931
that Labour might 'catch the wind of disgust which will blow
Mac and his friends out' (lines 21–2)?

d To what does Lansbury refer in lines 28–9 when he says 'the
movement . . . . will perish if once again it gets lost in the
morass of opportunism'?

5. The Ideas of the Socialist League

Those who have held radical and humanitarian views have counted
upon the pressure of the ever-widening democratic basis of the
electoral franchise to compel capitalism to yield better and better
the terms to the workers. In the pre-war period this theory of
5 gradual advance seemed plausible enough. With a growing national
prosperity, the national standard of living showed a steady rise.
Capitalism was ready to pay a price for its continued control in the
form of higher wages and fuller and better social services of all
kinds. During and immediately after the war this tendency became
10 more developed. The workers demonstrated their strength and
their power to protect capitalism with their lives and their labour;
their demands were satisfied so far as the capitalists considered it
economically possible, but always with the reservation that nothing must be done to deprive capitalism of its effective power of
15 control, whether in the financial economic or political sphere.

As soon as it became apparent that the limit of concession was
being reached and that, with a growing slump in world trade,
capitalism would break down under the burden it had taken upon
itself in more prosperous times, an immediate halt was called; the
20 National Government was formed to protect capitalism and to
bring about a rapid reversal of the progress by the withdrawal of
the concessions which had been made to the workers. It was
essential that the Government should be called National, as other-

wise it might have occurred to the great mass of the electorate that
25 it was merely a device to stabilise capitalism and not, as was
claimed for it, a means to save the country. . . .

From the moment when the Labour Government takes control
rapid and effective action must be possible in every sphere of the
national life. It will not be easy to detect the machinations of the
30 capitalists, and, when discovered, there must be means ready to
hand by which they can be dealt with promptly. The greatest
danger point will be the financial and credit structure of the country
and the Foreign Exchange position. We may liken the position that
will arise somewhat to that which arose in August 1914, but with
35 this difference, that at the beginning of the war the capitalists,
though very nervous and excited, were behind the Government to
a man, whereas when the Socialist Government takes office they
will not only be nervous and excited but against the Government to
a man. The Government's first step will be to call Parliament
40 together at the earliest possible date and place before it an Emergency Powers Bill to be passed through all its stages in one day.
This Bill would be wide enough in its terms to allow all that will be
immediately necessary to be done by ministerial orders. These
orders must be incapable of challenge in the Courts or in any way
45 except in the House of Commons.

This Bill must be ready in draft beforehand, together with the
main orders that will be made immediately upon its becoming law.

It is probable that the passage of this Bill will raise in its most
acute form the constitutional crisis.

> From: Stafford Cripps, 'Can Socialism Come By Constitu-
> tional Means?' in Cripps (ed.) *Problems of a Socialist Govern-*
> *ment*, Victor Gollancz, 1933, pp. 37–8. 42–3.

Questions

a Explain Cripps' idea that 'in the pre-war period this theory of
   gradual advance seemed plausible enough' (lines 4–5).
b What does Cripps mean when he says 'the National Government was formed to protect Capitalism and to bring about a
   rapid reversal of the progress by the withdrawal of the concession which had been made to the workers' (lines 19–22)?
c What danger does Cripps anticipate a new Labour Government
   would face on taking office (lines 27–39)?
d In Cripps's opinion, how should a Socialist Government neut-
   ralise such a capitalist's threat?
e To what possibilities might Cripps be alluding when he makes
   the supposition 'that the passage of this Bill will raise in most
   acute form the constitutional crisis (lines 48–9)?

6. A Falling-Out Among Thieves – Snowden Castigates MacDonald, 1934

At the last General Election millions of Labour, Liberal and free trade votes were given to the National Government candidates – because the electors believed Mr Baldwin's statement that free trade and protection were not the issue at the election. Now the
5 Government were boasting that they had killed free trade and established tariffs for a generation to come. He had been betrayed. That mattered little, but the country had been betrayed, and millions of electors who trusted to the statements of the party leaders had lost their confidence in the faith and honesty of their
10 political leaders. . . .

The Trust is that the Tories have got the power, and they mean to use it. At the next election the slogan will be National Government or Socialist Government. At that election the Tories will have no use for the Prime Minister except as an exhibition on Tory
15 platforms. . . . as a one-time Socialist who has seen the error of his ways, and has found salvation and his spiritual home in the Tory Party. He will be used for the same purpose as the reformed drunkard is used at the temperance meeting (Laughter). The Prime Minister told us at a recent meeting that he stood by everything he
20 had said as a Socialist. Let him act upon that and then he will see what use his Tory colleagues will have for him. He told us in the same speech that what the country needs is honest political leadership. I quite agree.

> Philip Snowden's speech in the House of Lords, reported by *The Times*, 4 July 1934.

Questions

a Why did Snowden feel that 'the country had been betrayed' (line 7)?

b How does Snowden foresee MacDonald being used in the next election?

c What did happen to MacDonald in the 1935 General Election?

d On what issues, apart from that of free trade, might critics question the honesty of the 'political leadership' (lines 22–3) of the National Government?

7. Labour's Unofficial Voice on Unemployment

I ask you Hon. Members opposite to tell me what they think these (unemployed) people can do. You have deprived them of any voice anywhere. You have established 7000 officials (in the distressed areas) without the slightest responsibility to the people, and we
5 cannot control them here. What do Hon. Members suggest they

should do? Vote every four or five years? I am not going to use exaggerated language, but I hope that if the Regulations which we brought in worsen the conditions of the people in my district, they will behave in such a manner that you will require to send a regular
10 army to keep order ('Shame'). I say that without the slightest hesitation.

I say quite frankly – I am weighing my words carefully – that there is only one way in which Hon. Members opposite can be brought to reason, and that is by trouble outside, because argu-
15 ments inside The House has failed to move them. If Income Tax is under consideration, these benches are packed. If there is some opposition to a little municipal Bill for which Hon. Members have been subsidised by private concerns, these benches are packed, but if it is the poor, they are empty. There is only one way in which the
20 poor can make their voice heard here and that is by making trouble outside.

> From a speech by Aneurin Bevan in The House of Commons, Hansard, Vol. 313, June 1936, quoted by J. Campbell, *Nye Bevan and the Mirage of British Socialism*, Weidenfeld & Nicolson, 1987, p. 55.

Questions

a   What was the policy of the National Government towards the unemployed in the distressed areas?
b   What action does Bevan suggest should be taken by the 'people in [his] district' (line 8)? How does this and lines 20–1, contrast with official labour policy on the issue?
c   What is Bevan's opinion of the sensitivity of 'the Hon. Members opposite' (line 1) to the problems of the poor?

8.   Bitter Labour Division on Sanctions, October 1935

Rt. Hon. George Lansbury, M.P. who was received with loud and prolonged applause said:

My own position has never shifted. I believe that force never has and never will bring permanent peace and permanent goodwill in
5 the world. I believe also that we in our Movement have really said that, in dealing with our own striving for Socialism. We have said to the workers: 'We are sorry for your plight, but you must wait until you have converted the rest of the people to your point of view'. I have gone into mining areas, I have gone into my own
10 district when people have been starving or semi-starving; I have stood in the midst of dockers who have been on the verge of

starvation (before there was any 'dole' or Poor Law Assistance, excepting the workhouse), and I have said to them 'No, you must not rise, you must have no violence, you must trust to the winning of this through public opinion'. I have never at any time said to the workers of this country: 'You must take up either arms, or sticks, or stones, in order to force your way to the end that you seek to attain'. . . .

I personally cannot see the difference between mass murder organised by the League of Nations, or mass murder organised between individual nations; to me it is exactly the same. . . .

It is said that people like me are irresponsible. I am no more irresponsible a leader than the greatest Trade Union leader in the country, I live my life as they do, amongst ordinary people, I see them when I am at home every day; I meet them and know all there is to know about them; and they do about me. But one thing I know is, that during the last war the youth, the early manhood of my division was slaughtered most terribly, and now I see the whole world rushing to perdition. I see us, as someone had said, rattling into barbarism again. If mine was the only voice in this Conference. . . . 'This is our faith, this is where we stand, and, if necessary, this is where we will die'.

Mr Ernest Bevin (Transport and General Workers' Union) said:

I hope you will carry no resolution of an emergency character telling a man with a conscience like Lansbury what he ought to do. If he finds that he ought to take a certain course, then this conscience should direct him as to the course he should take. It is placing the Executive and the Movement in an absolutely wrong position to be taking your conscience round from body to body asking to be told what you ought to do with it. There is one quotation from the Scriptures which George Lansbury has quoted today which I think he ought to apply to himself – 'Do unto others'. I have had to sit in Conference with the Leader and come to decisions, and I am a democrat and I feel we have been betrayed. . . .

People have been on this platform today talking about the destruction of capitalism. The middle classes are not doing too badly as a whole under capitalism and Fascism. Lawyers and members of other professions have not done too badly. The thing that is being wiped out is the Trade Union Movement. It is the only defence that the workers have got. Our Internationals have been broken; our Austrian brothers tried to defend themselves. We did all that we could. It is we who are being wiped out and who will be wiped out if Fascism comes here – the last vestige of defence that it has taken over 100 years to build up.

I feel that we have been let down. Every one of us on the General

Council of the TUC feel that we have been let down. We have had
enough of it during the last ten to twelve years as Trade Union
leaders – a very stiff time. I want to say to our friends who have
60 joined us in this political Movement, that our predecessors formed
this Party. It was not Keir Hardie who formed it, it grew out of the
bowels of the Trades Union Congress. It was a struggle for status
and equality, for Labour representation leading ultimately to
power, and none of us have ever 'ratted'. Whether we have won or
65 lost, we have taken our corner. . . .

They say he who takes the sword shall perish by the sword. The
man who has taken the sword is Mussolini and because Mussolini
has taken the sword we stand by the Scriptural doctrine and say
that he shall perish by economic sanctions. . . . I ask you to give
70 tomorrow an almost unanimous vote, leaving it to those who
cannot accept the policy of this great Conference to take their own
course.

> From the Report of the Annual Labour Party Conference, 1
> October 1935, quoted by F. Bealey *The Social and Political
> Thought of the British Labour Party*, Weidenfeld & Nicolson,
> 1970, pp. 147–8.

Questions

a   Summarise George Lansbury's own position (lines 3–5) on
    foreign policy.
b   In what ways does Lansbury suggest he has consistently trans-
    lated his foreign policy attitudes to the domestic situation (first
    paragraph)?
c   What does Lansbury suggest about the origins of his detestation
    of war?
d   What is Bevin's attitude to Lansbury's speech? Why?
e   With what justification could Bevin argue that 'I feel that we
    [the Trade Union Movement] have been let down' (line 57)?
f   What did Bevin want the Conference to do? Was he successful
    in his plea?

9.   United Front

Unity of all sections of the working-class movement.

Unity in the struggle against Fascism, reaction and war, and
against the National Government.

Unity in the struggle for immediate demands and the return of
5 Labour Government on the next stage in the advance of working-
class power.

Unity through the removal of all barriers between sanctions of
the working-class movement, through the strengthening of trade

unionism and co-operation, through the adoption of a fighting
programme of mass struggle, through the democratisation of the
Labour Party and the trade union movement.

Unity through the framework of the Labour Party and the trade
unions.

> 'The Manifesto of the Socialist League, the Communist
> party and the ILP, February 1937', quoted by K. Laybourn,
> *The Labour Party, 1881–1951*, Alan Sutton, 1988, p. 116.

Questions

a What was the international context in which the United Front
  was formed?
b What was the exception to the United Front's commitment to
  the struggle against 'reaction and war' (lines 2–3)?
c What evidence is there in this manifesto of a commitment to
  non-parliamentary methods for ensuring working-class power?
d What was the attitude of the Labour leadership and the Parliamentary Labour Party to the United Front?

10. A Left Wing Assault on Front Bench Betrayal of Socialism

We have heard in the constituencies and here that it is foolish for us
to oppose armaments and yet ourselves to adopt a policy for the
furtherance of which armaments are necessary, and that if we
succeeded in preventing the government from having arms we
should be helpless in the face of possible Fascist aggression. When
this Movement is strong enough to deny arms to the Capitalist
Government, it ceases to be a Government until those who are able
to deny them are themselves strong enough to form a Government;
and when that happens the Movement has declared – and I support
it, and my friends support it – that we are prepared to provide
whatever support is necessary to carry out a Socialist International
policy. But what we are not prepared to do is to tie the Movement
behind a National Government which will betray our policy. We
are not going to put a sword in the hands of our enemies that may
be used to cut off our own heads. . . .

If the immediate international situation is used as an excuse to get
us to drop our opposition to the rearmament programme of the
Government, the next phase must be that we must desist from any
industrial or political action that may disturb national unity in the
fact of Fascist aggression. Along that road is endless retreat, and at
the end of it a voluntary totalitarian state with ourselves erecting
the barbed wire around. You cannot collaborate, you cannot accept
the logic of collaboration on a first class issue like rearmament, and

at the same time evade the implication of collaboration all along the
25 line when the occasion demands it. Therefore, the Conference is
not merely discussing foreign policy; it is discussing the spiritual
and physical independence of the Working-Class Movement in this
country!

> From a speech by Aneurin Bevan, Labour Party Annual
> Conference Report 1937, quoted by J. Campbell, *Nye Bevan
> and the Mirage of British Socialism*, Weidenfeld & Nicolson,
> 1987, pp. 76–7.

Questions

a What is Bevan's attitude towards the National Government in
the first paragraph?
b To what 'Fascist aggression' (line 20) is Bevan referring?
c What does Bevan believe to be the logical outcome of
'desist[ing] from any industrial or political action that may
disturb national unity in the face of Fascist aggression' (lines
18–20)?
d What was the attitude of the Labour leadership to the 'rearmament programme of the Government' (lines 17–18) in 1937
against which Bevan railed?

11. Attlee in the Munich Debate

The fact is that in the game of power politics this country and
France have received a great defeat. I am not saying that this is all
due to the present Prime Minister.

5 The seeds of the present situation were sown long ago by the
Chancellor of the Exchequer, they were watered by the present
Home Secretary, and tended by the whole of this great National
Government. Seven years of National Government have brought
us to a day of humiliation, to a more dangerous position and a more
10 humiliating position than any that we have occupied since the days
of Charles II.

The moral of this is that the day when our policy changed, when
we left the path of collective security in the League of nations,
when we abandoned the attempt to make peace through the League
and under collective security, that day we took a step towards war.

15 What are we offered now? All we are offered now by the Prime
Minister is to push on with rearmament. Well, the people have seen
the gas masks, they have seen the trenches. They have fear in their
hearts, and as long as you follow this hopeless policy of power
politics, you will never lift this fear of war from the people.

20 In these bad days, there are, I believe, two things from which we
may draw some comfort. One was the resolution and calm of our

own people in this crisis. I believe that the Prime Minister must
have been able to bring to Herr Hitler – I hope he did – some sense
of the resolution of the people of this country, because it is one of
25 the dangers of the situation that the idea has gone abroad that this is
a decadent country. . . .

The second thing from which we may draw some comfort – and
this again, I hope, has gone home to the Dictators – is that
everywhere throughout the world there is utter hatred and detesta-
30 tion of war.

I believe that is as strong in Germany and in Italy as it is in this
country, and I think that now is the time when an effort should be
made to meet the real desires of the people of the world to redress
the balance against the rulers.

35 If the method we have been pursuing hitherto is pursued, sooner
or later we shall be in the abyss, for we have been looking down an
abyss in the last few days. This is not the time for four-Power
pacts, for new alliances, for power politics.

This is the time for a new peace conference and an all-in peace
40 conference. Let us call in the good offices of the United States of
America, and let us not exclude the Union of Soviet Socialist
Republics. I pleaded many months ago in this house that we
wanted a Press conference before the next war, but then I did not
assume that the next war would be complete defeat, and that is why
45 the Munich Conference was not a real peace conference. It was only
the delivery of an armistice.

I want a real conference, a peace conference to which people will
not come merely to rattle the sabre. I want a peace conference
which will endeavour to deal with the causes of war that are
50 affecting this world, the wrongs of the Versailles Treaty, the
wrongs of minorities, to deal with the colonial question, to deal
with the question of raw materials, to deal, above all, with the great
economic question, the condition-of-the-people question.

I believe, that today, if the world can take a lesson from
55 the events of these months, despite the sacrifice of the Czech
people, there is an opportunity of going forward to build a new
world.

A speech in the House of Commons by Clement Attlee,
Hansard, 3 October 1938, c 339, pp. 64–5.

Questions

a To what change in policy does Attlee attribute the move
towards war?
b Of what, according to Attlee, does Chamberlain's foreign
policy consist in the aftermath to Munich?
c In Attlee's view what are the 'two things from which we may
draw some comfort' (lines 20–1)?

d What hope does Attlee have of the situation in Germany and Italy? What do you think he might anticipate happening within those two countries?

e What is Attlee's solution to the crisis whose severity threatened the 'abyss' (line 36)? What differentiates this policy from that of the Munich conference? In what ways is it a distinctly Labour solution?

VII Labour as War-time Partners, 1940–45

Churchill's Government was hastily constructed at a time of national crisis, and the new Prime Minister sought to make his Cabinet a true reflection of resultant united national resolve; he rewarded Labour for its support of a change of administration and for its evident strength in the country by bringing Attlee and Greenwood into the War Cabinet of five, by making Bevin Minister of Labour (a vital position in the war effort and one soon to be recognised by War Cabinet status), and by finding ministerial places for Morrison (as Home Secretary), Jowitt, Alexander and Dalton. During the five years that Labour belonged to the Churchill government changes naturally occurred; in 1942 Attlee became deputy Prime Minister, Dalton moved to the Board of Trade, Cripps – still excluded from the official Labour Party – was drafted into the administration as Lord Privy Seal, and Greenwood resigned.

Labour's role in that Government during the war was an important one. By and large the military and foreign spheres of war planning were conducted by Churchill and Eden, although Attlee and Cripps (for a time Ambassador to Russia and falsely credited by the public with bringing the Soviets into the war against Hitler) were certainly involved in discussing strategy. It was on the home front that Labour came into its own. The Party – leaders and led – saw the inevitable corollaries of war – the planning, the public control, the emergence of all-powerful regional commissioners who controlled everything from fuel to labour, the egalitarianism – as precedents for the creation of a peace-time socialist state. Churchill was both concerned with winning the war and suspicious of socialist nostrums; it was Attlee, Dalton, Morrison – Labour ministers – who pressed and chivvied for constructive planning for a post-war world. After the threat of imminent destruction in 1940 and 1941 had been lifted and particularly after the tide had turned in late 1942 with the first of a sequence of allied victories against the Nazis, even Churchill could – occasionally – be persuaded to consider reconstruction. Dalton below describes a Cabinet Meeting which was buoyed up by one of those bursts of Churchillian enthusiasm for regenerating a country. He appointed a Minister of Reconstruction – Lord Woolton – after Labour pressure in

November 1943 but, in truth, the Prime Minister hovered on the issue, preferring to win the war first. Consequently, while some things were done (for example, the Means Test was abolished) and some plans were laid (for health, for education, for distribution of industry and for Town and Country Planning) – usually, but not always, drawn up under the aegis of Labour ministers – overall, the rate at which social reconstruction was effected was a considerable disappointment to Labour back benchers.

This can be seen in the divisions over the Beveridge Report in February 1943. Beveridge, a Liberal planner, whose ideas were formed when working on social reform for Lloyd George before 1914, had been commissioned by Greenwood to report on the social services; in many senses, his report harked back to those Liberal principles of 1911, assuming the continued working of capitalism and embracing the principle of flat rate contributions, but its vision of a nation freed forever of disease, want, squalor, ignorance and idleness captured the public imagination. In the Commons debate that February, the government spokesmen (Anderson and Wood) were unenthusiastic and unconvincing. The Parliamentary Labour Party defied its leaders, putting down and voting on an official amendment to the government motion by calling for legislation as a matter of urgency. Ninety-seven Labour MPs voted against the government. It was the biggest division of the war. It identified the Labour party publicly as the champion of social reform. It demonstrated, too, the difficulties faced by Labour's leaders in retaining loyalty to a national government formed to win the war whilst at the same time trying to retain the loyalty of the rank and file.

Bevan, a back-bencher, was the most outspoken and consistent of critics; under his editorship, *The Tribune* emerged as one of the only periodicals which dared to challenge war strategy and leadership. Bevan became increasingly 'a squalid nuisance' in the judgement of the Prime Minister for the persistence of his vitriolic attacks. But the Welshman was catholic in his opposition sorties; he led a significant ambush of the government in March 1943, mustering 61 votes for an immediate rise in old age pensions, and he was almost expelled from the Party in April 1944 when he made a ferocious assault on Ernest Bevin's Mines Legislation imposing penalties of up to five years' imprisonment for those taking part in, or instigating, unofficial strikes. Conservatives must have been wryly amused by such dissension between two Labour politicians both claiming to represent the interests of working men. Indeed, internecine struggle between certain individuals within the party is a characteristic of the period; Bevan and Bevin roundly loathed each other in these years, and Bevin felt equally strongly about the ambitious Morrison who sniped at Attlee consistently until after the 1945 election victory. Professor Harold Laski, left-wing intellectual and Chairman of the Labour Party Executive, was publicly and damagingly critical of Clement Attlee, especially in 1945. It is therefore a sign of the Labour leader's very real quality that he succeeded in harmonising these discordant elements in the Labour Cabinet after the war.

Attlee's role in the war-time government deserves special mention. He effectively ran domestic affairs; he chaired almost every subcommittee set up to consider Home Front legislation and planning; and he had the courage, even audacity (see below) to tell Churchill some uncomfortable home truths. He proved when deputising for the Prime Minister to be an extremely effective Cabinet chairman. His unflashy and unflappable manner, his competence and his moderacy infuriated some ('he brings to the fierce struggle of politics the tepid enthusiasm of a lazy summer afternoon at a cricket match' said Bevan), but probably helped convince many electors in July 1945 that his party was responsible and trustworthy.

The National Government ended in May 1945 after agreement had failed to be reached on the timing of the next election – after victory in the war against Japan (Churchill) or in October (Attlee). A date was set for 5 July instead, and Churchill soldiered on for a couple of months with a caretaker Cabinet.

Labour published an election programme, 'Let us Face the Future', which called for selective nationalisation, full employment and improved social services. Churchill unsuccessfully attempted to dub his recent allies 'closet Bolsheviks'. Attlee, dogged by the pedantic socialist constitutionalism of Laski, was nevertheless the embodiment of reasonableness. Very few (apart from Gallup Poll) accurately forecast a result rendered unpredictable by an outdated electoral register and by the large number of service men and women overseas. There had been some straws in the wind – during the war, independent socialists who broke the party truce, contested and won several by-elections – but appearances suggested a triumph for the war leader. Yet, as A. J. P. Taylor puts it, 'the electors cheered Churchill and voted against him'. When the election results emerged three weeks after voting, Labour had won a handsome victory, 393 seats to the Conservative's 213, and had secured an overall majority of 146, thus for the first time ensuring real political power. This sea change had occurred partly because the Conservatives were blamed for pre-war appeasement, unemployment and Means Test policies, partly because Labour had proved itself in war-time government and in its enthusiasm for reconstruction, and partly because the Liberals had at last been erased as an effective party on the Left. Now Labour could apparently look forward with confidence to a prolonged and constructive period of office.

1. A Labour Vision in 1940

The people of this country and Europe are not prepared to lose
their lives in order to reassemble a ramshackle Europe. They are
looking to higher ideals than that. . . . It is not enough to offer to
the people of Belgium, France and this country merely the defence
5   of the institutions of democracy against the threats of Nazi dictatorship, because they recognise that, after all, it is that sort of
democracy that brought Europe to war. If we are to persuade
them, to enthuse them and inspire them with the defence of
democracy, the conception of democracy has to be fitted into
10   modern needs. We have to fill it up with a greater social content.
    Sometimes the Prime Minister's car is too sensitively attuned to
the bugle notes of Blenheim for him to hear the whisperings in the
streets. . . . In many respects the Prime Minister is not being well
advised. . . . We on this side of the House are deeply anxious that
15   the Government should adopt a policy bold, visionary and inspir-
ing to try and associate ordinary men and women spiritually and
not merely formally with the war effort. If that can be done, we
shall get a response which will amaze even the Prime Minister with
his faith.

    From a speech by Aneurin Bevan, House of Commons, 8
    October 1940, *Hansard*, Vol. 365, cols 345–50.

Questions

a   In what war-time context was this speech made? Why, then,
    might its content be considered significant?
b   To what 'higher ideals' (line 3) does Bevan believe 'the people of
    this country and Europe' (line 1) were looking?
c   Explain Bevan's 'conception of democracy' (line 9).
d   What does Bevan mean when he says 'the Prime Minister's car
    is too sensitively attuned to the bugle notes of Blenheim for him
    to hear the whisperings in the streets' (lines 11–13)
e   For what did those 'on this side of the House' (line 14) call from
    the government?

2. Reconstruction

(a) Labour's voice in the War Cabinet

I doubt whether in your inevitable and proper preoccupation with
military problems you are fully cognisant of the extent to which
decisions must be taken and implemented in the field of post-war
reconstruction before the end of the war. It is not that persons of
5   particular political views are seeking to make vast changes. These
changes have already taken place. The changes from peacetime to

wartime industry, the concentration of industry, the alterations in
trade relations with foreign countries and with the Empire, to
mention only a few factors, necessitate great readjustments and
10 new departures in the economic and industrial life of the nation.
When you speak of men returning to their jobs as one of the first
essentials at the end of the war I agree, but without planning there
won't be the jobs. . . .

. . . .the doctrines set out in your note to me would destroy all
15 hope of this country playing an effective part in carrying the world
through the difficult period of transition.

I am certain that unless the Government is prepared to be
outrageous in planning for peace as it has been in carrying on the
war, there is extreme danger of disaster when the war ends. I doubt
20 if any of our colleagues who have been giving attention to post-war
problems would be content with the mere preparation of paper
schemes.

I do not think the people of this country especially the fighting
men would forgive us if we failed to take decisions to implement
25 them because of some constitutional inhibition. I am not concerned
at the moment with the Beveridge Report and its merits or
demerits, but with the general principle. . . . My contention is that
if, as I think is generally agreed, it is not possible at the present time
to have a general election the Government and the present House of
30 Commons must be prepared to take responsibility not only for
winning the war but for taking the legislative and administrative
action which is thought necessary for the post-war situation.

> Note from Attlee to Churchill, February 1943, quoted in
> Kenneth Harris, *Attlee*, Weidenfeld & Nicolson, 1982,
> pp. 220–21.

Questions

a According to Attlee, what 'changes have already taken place'
   (line 6) in the war?
b Why, then, does Attlee argue that planning for a post-war
   world is necessary?
c To what 'extreme danger of disaster' (line 19) might Attlee be
   referring here?
d What 'general principle' (line 27) is exercising Attlee in this
   passage?
e What does that passage reveal about the contrasting priorities
   and interests of Attlee and Churchill?

(b) A Prime Minister converted?

A most remarkable and surprisingly good and important Cabinet.
The P.M. has issued a short Note on War – Transition – Peace. In

this he argues that we should fail completely in our duty if we had not got ready, before the German war ends, complete schemes for the Transition Period, during which we should ensure for all our people Food and Employment. The Transition Period he proposes to define as either two years from the defeat of Germany or four years from 1st January 1944, whichever ends first. He is anxious to speed up all preparations now being made. There is also circulated a paper by the Prof., listing a large range of topics on which decision will be necessary. Quite a surprising number of them fall within my Departmental field, either wholly or partly.

Very great credit is due to Attlee and, in a lesser degree to Morrison, for having brought about this remarkable change in the P.M.'s attitude. They have both been having a great go at him, and tonight the P.M. who is in a very good temper and great spirits, says that he has now been led to see this question quite differently. He says that this is because he has been 'jostled and beaten up, by the Deputy Prime Minister'. For this, he says, he is very grateful. The Transition has now taken a very firm shape in his mind. We shall not pass direct from war to peace, even apart from the complication of the two-stage ending of war. Between these two there must be a transition for which it is our duty to make most careful preparation now, and we should rule out nothing important for the simple needs of the Transition, merely because it is controversial. He then elaborates, with great dramatic detail, how we should prepare a great book, the Book of Transition, like the War Book, running to perhaps a thousand closely printed pages or taking the form of a number of Reports and precise plans contained in drawers, one above another, so that, if any amateurish critic says, 'You have no plan for this or that', it would be easy to pull out a drawer, bring out a paper and say, 'Here it all is. . . .' There follows a few casual references to the next general election, whereon the P.M. is a bit cautious, saying it all depends on whether the parties break up or hold together; that if we hold together we shall be more masters of our fate, but that if we break up, he, assuming he continued P.M. would not feel able to delay more than a month or two an appeal to the country.

This Cabinet, in short, went very well. I spoke afterwards with Attlee and congratulated him on the success of his efforts. He said there had been a frightful row last week, and loud explosions from the P.M. But now that the smoke had cleared away, the P.M. having invited various Tory ministers, including Butler and Crookshank, to this meeting – they had both been dumb through-out – had now led the Tory troops through the breach which we had made in their defences. I told Attlee that it was nonsense for ministers without departments or staffs – to try to deputise for or try to compete with people like myself who had large staffs working on these post-war problems. I therefore counted on being

50   effectively in the picture when the new drive began. He expressed
strong agreement with this view and asked me to send him a note
on the whole matter.

> Hugh Dalton, 21 October 1943, from B. Pimlott (ed.) *The
> Second World War Diary of Hugh Dalton*, Jonathan Cape,
> 1986, pp. 655–7.

Questions

a What is the Prime Minister's vision of Transition as retold by
   Dalton?
b To whom does Dalton give the credit for Churchill's conversion? How was this conversion achieved?
c What are the Prime Minister's views at this time of the next
   General Election?
d Explain Dalton's meaning when he writes that 'the P.M. . . . .
   had now led the Tory troops through the breach which we had
   made in their defences' (lines 42–6).
★ e How far were the Transition policies enunciated by Churchill in
   this Cabinet actually executed during the remainder of the war?
   How constant did Churchill personally remain to this enthusiasm recorded here?
f What impression do you get of Dalton himself from the last few
   lines of this passage?

3. The Deputy Prime Minister Rebukes his Leader

Prime Minister

I have for some time had it in mind to write to you on the method
or rather lack of method of dealing with matters requiring Cabinet
decisions. The proceeding last night (Wednesday) at the Cabinet
have brought matters to a head. I consider the present position
5   inimical to the successful performance of the tasks imposed upon us
as a Government and injurious to the war effort. I am stating the
views I hold bluntly and frankly as I consider that it is my duty to
do so. I am sure you will not resent plain speaking. My complaint
relates mainly but not wholly to the method of dealing with civil
10   affairs. I quite understand that, occupied so heavily as you are with
the military conduct of the war, it is not possible for you to give as
much attention as you would wish to civil affairs. But, that being
so, I should have thought that you would have reposed some
confidence in your Cabinet colleagues, but on the contrary you
15   exhibit a very scanty respect for their views.

You have set up a number of committees over some of which I
have the honour to preside to deal with various aspects of our

affairs. They have been framed by you to give a fair representation
of political opinion and to bring to bear on particular subjects the
minds of Ministers of experience. Other ministers when matters
concerning their departments are convinced are summoned to
attend.

I doubt if you realise the length of time and the amount of work
entailed on busy ministers not only by attendance at these
committees, but by reading the relevant papers and seeking advice
from persons of knowledge. No one grudges the time and labour,
provided that the work done bears fruit, but it must be recognised
that the strain of a long war inevitably begins to tell on Ministers. If
to this is added exasperation and a sense of frustration, the tension
becomes great. At these committees we endeavour and I claim with
marked success to reach agreement and to subordinate party views
to the general interest. It is quite exceptional for Party issues to
arise. The conclusion of the Committees are brought to the Cabinet
in memoranda which we try to keep as short as possible in an
attempt to save members the trouble of reading long disquisitions.
What happens then?

Frequently a long delay before they can be considered. When
they do come before the Cabinet it is very exceptional for you to
have read them. More and more often you have not read even the
note prepared for your guidance. Often half an hour and more is
wasted in explaining what could have been grasped by two or three
minutes reading of the document. Not infrequently a phrase
catches your eye which gives rise to a disquisition on an interesting
point only slightly connected with the subject matter. The result is
long delays and unnecessarily long Cabinets imposed on Ministers
who have already done a full day's work and who will have more
to deal with before they get to bed.

I will give two recent instances.

Instead of assuming that agreement having been reached, there is
a prima facie case for the proposal, it is assumed that it is due to the
malevolent intrigues of socialist Ministers who have beguiled their
weak Conservative colleagues. This suggestion is unjust and
insulting to Ministers of both Parties.

But there is something worse than this. The conclusions agreed
upon by a Committee on which have sat five or six members of the
Cabinet and other experienced Ministers are then submitted to the
Lord Privy Seal and the Minister of Information, two Ministers
without Cabinet responsibility neither of whom has given any
serious attention to the subject. Time and again important matters
are delayed or passed in accordance with the decision of the Lord
Privy Seal. The excuse is given that in him you have the mind of
the Conservative Party. With some knowledge of opinion in the
Conservative Party in the House as expressed to me on the
retirement from and re-entry into the Government of Lord

65   Beaverbrook I suggest that this view would be indignantly
      repudiated by the vast majority. There is a serious constitutional
      issue here. In the eyes of the country and under our constitution the
      eight members of the War Cabinet take responsibility for decisions.
      I have myself assured members of both Parties who have been
70   disturbed by the influence of the Lord Privy Seal that this was so.
      But if the present practice continues I shall not be able to do so in
      the future.
         I have spoken very frankly on these discontents. I have written
      on my own account, but I am well aware that I am expressing
75   much that is in the minds of many colleagues in the Government
      whether Conservative, Labour, Liberal or independent.
            A letter from C. R. Attlee to Winston Churchill, 19 January
            1945, quoted by Kenneth Harris, *Attlee*, Weidenfeld &
            Nicolson, 1982, pp. 241–3.

Questions

a   In what ways did Churchill's dealing with the committee's
    conclusions, brought to Cabinet, cause 'exasperation and a sense
    of frustration' (line 29) in the committee Ministers and Attlee?
b   How, according to Attlee, did Churchill reveal his distrust of
    socialist members of the administration?
c   Of what constitutional impropriety does Attlee complain in
    lines 54–72.
d   What does this letter reveal both about the relations between
    Attlee and Churchill and about Attlee's position in the war-time
    administration?

4.   The Election Campaign – Two Labour Voices

(a) *Bevan*

It is for us a question of where power is going to lie. There is no
absence of knowledge, there is no lack of wisdom, as to what to do
in Great Britain. What is lacking is that the power lies in the wrong
hands and the will to do it is not there.

5   We want to tell our friends on the other side that the men in the
Services are not going to allow a repetition of what happened
between the wars. We are not going to allow our financial resources
to be sent all over the world, and idleness and starvation to exist in
Great Britain. And we warn them that we are entering this fight
10   with this in our hearts. We were brought up between the two wars
in the distressed areas of this country, and we have such biting and
bitter memories as will never be erased until the Tories are
destroyed on every political platform in this country. . . .
         It is in no pure Party spirit that we are going into this election.

15   We know that in us, and in us alone, lies the economic salvation of
     this country and the opportunity of providing a great example to
     the world. Therefore, remember, in the elections that lie immedi-
     ately ahead, we are the memories of those bitter years; we are the
     voice of the British people; we are the natural custodians of the
20   interests of those young men and women in the Services abroad.
     We have been the dreamers, we have been the sufferers, and we are
     the builders. We enter this campaign at this general election, not
     merely to get rid of the Tory majority – that will not be enough for
     our task. It will not be sufficient to get a parliamentary majority.
25   We want the complete political extinction of the Tory Party, and
     twenty five years of Labour Government. We cannot do in five
     years what requires to be done. It needs a new industrial
     revolution. We require that modern industrial science be applied to
     our heavy industry. It can only be done by men and modern minds,
30   by men of a new age. It can only be done by the fine young men
     and women that we have seen in this Conference this week.
               Speech by Bevan, Labour Party Conference May 1945,
               Labour Party Annual Conference Report, 1945, pp. 130–2,
               quoted by J. Campbell, *Nye Bevan and the Mirage of British
               Socialism*, Weidenfeld & Nicolson, 1987, p. 140.

(b) Attlee

When I listened to the Prime Minister's speech last night, in which
he gave such a travesty of the policy of the Labour Party, I realised
at once what was his object. He wanted the electors to understand
35   how great was the difference between Winston Churchill the Great
     Leader in war of a united nation and Mr Churchill, the Party Leader
     of the Conservatives. He feared lest those who had accepted his
     leadership in war might be tempted out of gratitude to follow
     him further. I thank him for having disillusioned them so
40   thoroughly. . . .
     Forty years ago the Labour Party might with some justice have
     been called a class Party, representing almost exclusively the wage
     earner. It is still based on organised labour but has steadily become
     more and more inclusive. . . .
45   The Conservative Party remains as always a class Party. In
     twenty years in the House of Commons I cannot recall more than
     half a dozen from the ranks of the wage earners. It represents today,
     as in the past, the forces of property and privilege. The Labour
     Party is, in fact, the one Party which most nearly reflects in its
50   representation and composition all the main streams which flow
     into the great river of our national life. . . .
     Our appeal to you, therefore, is not narrow or sectional. We are
     proud of the fact that our country in the hours of its great danger
     stood firm and united, setting an example to the world of how a

great democratic people rose to the height of the occasion and saved
democracy and liberty. We are proud of the self–sacrifice and
devotion displayed by men and women in every walk of life in this
great adventure.

We call you to another great adventure which will demand the
same high qualities as those shown in the war; the adventure of
civilisation. . . .

We have to plan the broad lines of our national life so that all may
have the duty and the opportunity of rendering service to the
nation, everyone in his or her sphere, and that all may help to create
and share in an increasing material prosperity free from the fear of
want. We have to preserve and enhance the beauty of our country
to make it a place where men and women may live finely and
happily free to worship God in their own way, free to speak their
minds, free citizens of a great country.

> From an election broadcast on BBC radio by C. R. Attlee, 5
> June 1945, quoted by Kenneth Harris, *Attlee*, Weidenfeld &
> Nicolson, 1982, pp. 256–8.

Questions

a Against 'a repetition of what [that] happened between the wars'
does Bevan warn his audience in lines 6–7 of Extract (a)?

b Compare and contrast the attitude of both politicians to their
Conservative opponents.

c In what ways is Attlee's appeal 'not narrow or sectional'
(Extract b, line 52)?

d What visions of the future are sketched out by Bevan and
Attlee? How similar are they?

5. Let Us Face the Future

The Labour Party is a Socialist Party, and proud of it. Its ultimate
purpose at home is the establishment of the Socialist Commonwealth of Great Britain – free, democratic, efficient, progressive,
public-spirited, its material resources organised in the service of the
British people.

But Socialism cannot come overnight, as the product of a
weekend revolution. The members of the Labour Party, like the
British people, are practical-minded men and women.

There are basic industries ripe and over-ripe for public ownership and management in the direct service of the nation. There are
many smaller businesses rendering good service which can be left
to go on with their useful work.

There are big industries not yet ripe for public ownership which
must nevertheless be required by constructive supervision to

15　further the nation's needs and not to prejudice national interests by restrictive anti-social monopoly or cartel agreements – caring for their own capital structures and profits at the cost of a lower standard of living for all. . . .

20　The Labour Party has played a leading part in the long campaign for proper social security for all – social provision against rainy days, coupled with economic policies calculated to reduce rainy days to a minimum. Labour led the fight against the mean and shabby treatment which was the lot of millions while Conservative Governments were in power over long years. A Labour Govern-

25　ment will press on rapidly with legislation extending social insurance over the necessary wide field to all.

But great national programmes of education, health and social services are costly things. Only an efficient and prosperous nation can afford them in full measure. If, unhappily, bad times were to

30　come, and our opponents were in power, then, running true to form, they would be likely to cut these social provisions on the plea that the nation could not meet the cost. That was the line they adopted on at least three occasions between the wars.

There is no good reason why Britain should not afford such

35　programmes, but she will need full employment and the highest possible industrial efficiency in order to do so. . . .

The Labour Party is essentially a democratic party. It seeks to attain its purpose by persuasion, and not by violence, and to maintain that right to full freedom of criticism and association

40　without which human life is deprived of dignity and fullness. Labour takes the view that political democracy cannot be a reality without economic democracy. It seeks to establish a free and prosperous society of equals, and believes that the highroad to such a society lies through the gateway of Socialism. . . .

45　Because it is a Socialist Party, the Labour Party believes in the brotherhood of man. The advance of science has bound the peoples of the world together by a thousand ties. It has also produced instruments of destruction so potent that the institution of war has become incompatible with the survival of civilisation. The Labour

50　Party regards war as senseless and wicked, a blasphemy against the human spirit. It detests national and racial as much as class barriers. The Socialists' faith is as passionately opposed to international anarchy as it is to economic anarchy. It recognises that both spring from the fundamental and incurable anarchy of Capitalism.

55　The Labour Party believes that the only final guarantee of peace lies in the development of a Co-operative World Commonwealth of Nations. The League of Nations can succeed only in proportion as it develops in the direction of world government. Planning and control in international life both postulate and follow from national

60　planning and socialised control of our national life. A foreign policy directed to establishing a Co-operative World Commonwealth of

Nations is the inevitable corollary to a home policy which actively works for the establishment of the Socialist State. Such a foreign policy is the only effective alternative to the present drift toward another world war.

> From 'Let us Face the Future', Labour Party Statement of Policy, April 1945, pp. 10, 13, 18, quoted by Frank Bealey, *The Social and Political Thought of the British Labour Party*, Weidenfeld & Nicolson, 1970, pp. 164–6.

Questions

a Against what policies of past Conservative governments are attacks made in this document?

b What limits are placed on wholesale implementation of the Labour Party's Clause 4 in the constitution of 1918?

c On the achievement of what economic conditions is 'proper social security for all' (line 20) predicated here?

d What echoes of past Labour foreign policy can you detect in lines 45–65? How far did the foreign policy of Bevin and Attlee between 1945 and 51 follow the principles enunciated in 'Let us Face the Future'?

6. Silent Revolution

Britain has undergone a silent revolution. Few suspected it. Hardly a politician from one end of the country to another had ventured to forecast what has happened at the polls. The people kept their secret, yet throughout the country, in country no less than in town they swung to the Left. And when they voted Left they meant it. They had no use for the middle-of-the-road Liberals; they voted Labour and they knew what they were voting for. The Conservative press had seen that they should know the worst; the Prime Minister had tried to scare them in broadcast after broadcast. But their marrows were not frozen; they took the risk.

The British vote parallels the revulsion of feeling that has occurred throughout Europe against old regimes and old habits of thought. There is encouragement in this, for if our affairs are wisely managed we have a magnificent chance of exerting British leadership in a desperately troubled world. Many of us, perhaps may have felt in advance a little apprehension at the thought of a Labour victory on the edge of the economic upheaval of demobilisation and with all the great problems of European and Far Eastern resettlement in front of us. A Labour Government will have the responsibility of carrying us through and we must give it all the support and loyalty we can. No Government has ever had a harder task before it in time of peace, but none has ever had a greater opportunity.

25   First thoughts are inevitably of the Government's defeat and what brought it about. The conclusions are salutary. Uppermost is the lesson that the British people will not be dominated by one man. They admire Mr Churchill as a great Englishman; they are grateful to the war leader, but they are resentful of the party
30   politician. It is now plain that Mr Churchill's broadcast and his attempt to turn the election into a personal plebiscite did him immense harm. As in President Roosevelt's elections the influence of the popular newspapers on political opinion is shown to be far less than their proprietors like to think; they cannot manufacture
35   opinion at their will. But what caused the revulsion of feeling? It can hardly be that Labour has won because of affection. The over-whelming influence was distrust of the Conservatives. This is not because of what they have done while they were in the Coalition but because of their history before 1940. Munich and the
40   'phoney war' have been too much to stomach, and even Mr Churchill has not been able to make people believe that there has been a change of heart. The Conservative record has been enough to wipe out the sentiment for a National Coalition, which again was evidently not as deep as many thought. Reactionary in social
45   and international policy before the war, the Conservative party held out no hope for the future. If reconstruction was to be bold, if the high hopes of full employment and social security were to be fulfilled, it was not the Conservatives who could be entrusted with the task. The soldiers' vote, in particular, went against them, but it
50   was only the reflection of the way the mass of the people at home were taking.

There are of course, some things in the election to be regretted. The submergence of the Liberal party is a disappointment. Given Proportional Representation, the party would still have a future,
55   but it is obvious that under the present system its hopes must be slender. The country will part with Mr Churchill with many regrets. After all, he is the greatest Prime Minister we have known since Gladstone and the greatest national leader since Pitt. But he has been the symbol of an attitude of mind against which the world
60   has turned. The new Labour Government will have new faces and may be in part scratch material. The first thing it will have to forget is the Coalition mind. Its leaders should know how much the Coalition Government, to say nothing of the minority Labour Governments of 1924 and 1929, lost by timidity and shilly-
65   shallying. They will keep the confidence of the country in the degree in which they show themselves to have purpose and conviction and are ready to accept the help of men of goodwill. They must rid themselves of their old inferiority complex, bring in fresh blood, and set out boldly. The country will not be afraid of its

70 first Socialist Government; the Government must not be afraid of the country which has made it.

> Leader in the *Guardian*, written by A. P. Wadsworth, Friday, 27 July 1945.

Questions

a With what justification could the author describe this as a 'revolution'?

b What 'apprehension' did many feel 'at the thought of a Labour victory' (lines 17–18)?

c What paradoxes in the public estimation of Winston Churchill does the author point up here?

d How does the author explain 'the revulsion of feeling' (line 35) against the Government?

e What 'things in the election [might] be regretted' (line 50) in the author's view?

f 'No Government has ever had a harder task before it in time of peace' (lines 22–3); how true was this? What does the author in lines 61–7 suggest Labour should do successfully to tackle that task?

VIII Majority Government at Last – Labour, 1945–51

The government of 1945–50 stands unchallenged as Labour's most successful period of administration. The strength and quality of the Cabinet, the edifice of legislative construction, and the wider sense in which it rewrote the ground rules of post-war government policy from welfare to industry have ensured that the first Attlee Government remains a yardstick against which all subsequent Labour Governments have been, and will be, compared. The leading figures of the administration were colourful, even heroic, although many of them were approaching old age, an approach hastened by the immense strains of government in this difficult period. Attlee, even if he himself could not be dubbed 'colourful', was an exceptional chairman, able to expedite government business and so make policy happen, skilled at retaining control of affairs even when the victim of sustained intrigue, and – deceptively 'ordinary' – the master of his party until 1951. Bevin became one of the great Foreign Secretaries of the century; Attlee wanted a trade unionist in the post, a master of negotiation, to deal with Russian and American diplomats, and Bevin proved to be an outstanding minister. Dalton, economic theorist and text-book writer, went to the Exchequer until his penchant for intrigue and gossip led him to an indiscretion in leaking Budget details to the Press in November 1947.

He was succeeded by Sir Stafford Cripps whose Christian asceticism and capacity to make of austerity a religious hybrid of crusade and mission made him a towering force in Cabinet and country until mortal illness struck him down at the end of this period. Nye Bevan, Churchill's scourge and 'squalid nuisance', was brought into the Cabinet, its youngest member, to channel his passionate socialism into the realisation of a great project, the building of the National Health Service. And the Home Secretary and Deputy Prime Minister was Herbert Morrison, manipulator of the party machine, architect of nationalisation, master tactician and fixer, whose personal ambition led him to conspire against Attlee, yet whose reading of the political pulse rendered him invaluable to the government.

With such a substantial majority and with the political initiative, it seemed as if Labour had the world at its feet. It was, however, constrained from the beginning by immense problems caused by the war; the legacy of victory was economic exhaustion, European devastation, colonial unrest and – something it took a decade fully to register – a diminished world standing in the era of the Super Powers. From the first month of office, Attlee's government faced the unpalatable consequences of victory, and of peace. The end of Lend-Lease, and so of American economic assistance, forced Attlee to employ Keynes to go cap in hand to Truman to ask for a loan in autumn 1945; it was the first of many such crises.

Despite laudable efforts to reduce imports by rationing (even bread was rationed from 1946) and to encourage exports, the country's economic state was fragile; commodity and material shortages, problems over manpower and demobilisation, the loss of overseas investments, and high defence expenditure, conspired to keep it that way. Economic performance was not helped by the savage winter of 1947, by coal reorganisation in 1946–7, and by intermittant strikes from 1947 onwards, especially in the docks. Persistent weakness manifested itself in the convertibility crisis of 1947, in the evident need for Marshall Aid, and in the devaluation of 1949. Perhaps the prolonged belt-tightening of the period – even though exports improved miraculously – cost the Labour Party its majority by 1951.

There was no warm after-glow from shared sacrifice and common purpose among the war-time allies; the Labour Government had swiftly to recognise the enormous difficulties inherent in dealing with Stalin, who seemed bent on European domination. The Cabinet's apprehension of the threat and of the need to draw in America as a bulwark against Soviet expansion was personified in the massive figure of Ernest Bevin. It was he who seized on America's offer of Marshall Aid and organised Europe to channel the resources; he, with Attlee, who precipitated the Truman doctrine by the decision to disengage from Greece and Turkey; he who was the architect of NATO in 1949, binding America and Canada into the defence of Western Europe after the siege of Berlin threatened war with Russia. He and Attlee were equally determined that Britain should have her own nuclear capability, and initiated the nuclear programme in such secrecy that the great majority of the Labour Cabinet knew nothing of its existence. Foreign policy divided the Labour Party more than did domestic issues; in April 1947 'Keep Left' was formed, a ginger group of the Left led by Crossman and Foot which campaigned against Britain's 'ganging-up' with America and against 'American Imperialism' more generally. The National Service Bill of 1947 enraged the pacifist Left of the party. And from 1950 involvement in the Korean war, with the consequent strain on national finances of dramatically increased defence expenditure, was at the root of Bevan's damaging and public resignation from the Cabinet. This illuminated Britain's difficulty; she might wish to remain a world power and exclusive member of the nuclear club, but increasingly she could not afford the resources to maintain a world military presence. In recognition of this, the Labour Government started the long retreat from empire. Attlee masterminded the process by which independence was given to India in 1947, replacing Wavell with his own choice – Mountbatten – giving his new Viceroy huge powers to settle the terms and shape of withdrawal, and putting a premium on speed at every stage. Where Labour's Indian policy has been praised by historians, few have been as generous about its stewardship of Palestine. Bevin was early convinced by Foreign Office Arabists that massive Jewish immigration to Palestine was unacceptable. His stolid pursuit of this policy has led him to be accused of anti-Semitism by some; certainly American Jews, Zionists in Britain, even the US administration believed him to be so. He saw the need for good Arab relations and the importance of oil to the west; others were more swayed by the Holocaust and the plight in 1945 of surviving Jewish refugees from Europe. The surrender of the mandate, the inaction of British forces in Palestine during the last months of occupation, and the apparent drift and uncertainty of British policy there reflected badly on the Labour Government.

It would be wrong to suggest that Labour's policies were determined entirely in reaction to events; it positively took legislative initiatives in seeking to realise that socialist vision of state support from cradle to grave, and of controlling the commanding heights in the economy. Social-welfare policy owed something to Beveridge, especially in the National Insurance Act, but the National Health Service was very much Nye Bevan's own conception. The National Health Act in fact rejected the Socialist Medical Association's blue-print for a locally-controlled service and for salaried doctors, and again was opposed vigorously from within the medical profession by GPs who saw their independence threatened; but Bevan proved more subtle and adaptive, less doctrinaire than his critics anticipated. Still, he believed passionately in the inviolability of the basic principle he had laid down, of a free universal health service; it was attacks on this from within the Cabinet after 1949, especially from Gaitskell who wanted prescription then spectacle and dental charges, which precipitated his resignation in 1951 and the Bevanite split of the 1950s.

The Attlee government changed the economic landscape by its implementation of a policy of nationalisation; only after 1979 has the possibility of freeing these industries from state control, of privatising, been countenanced, for up to that date there was a considerable cross-party support for the concept. Between 1946 and 1948 Labour nationalised coal mines, electricity, gas, the railways and the Bank of England. Thereafter, with Morrison calling for 'consolidation' and Bevan and the Left determined on further 'socialisation' embodied in the emotive issue of steel nationalisation, the momentum for public ownership slowed. Iron and steel were in fact nationalised in 1950. Morrison was a withering critic of the hastily compiled 'shopping list' of 1950 when the meat, water, cement and sugar industries were picked out for state control. It is unlikely that Labour gained electoral advantage from the commitment. Nevertheless, what had been achieved was momentous, and enabled Labour to think about planning for future investment and for the economy at large. Still – there were Labour critics who attacked the levels of compensation paid to former private owners (especially of coal), the employment of some of these employers on the new public boards, and the lack of workers' involvement in the management of the new nationalised industries.

Several factors probably explained the electoral disappointments of 1950–51. By 1950 the Conservatives had recovered from the shattering defeat of 1945 and, while accepting the permanence of some of Labour's heritage, sought successfully to attack first the harshnesses and deprivations which accompanied austerity, second, the shopping list of further targets, and third, the insufficiency of the housing programme. They were helped by Bevan's ill-judged 'vermin' speech and by Labour's own Redistribution Act which lost the party 30 crucial inner-city seats. Labour, indeed, won a majority of votes cast (3 per cent more than the Conservatives) but votes were piled up in safe Labour seats; in the new House, Labour had an overall majority of only 5. Harold Wilson and James Callaghan were later to show how effectively governments could govern with slender majorities, but Attlee's administration was now aged and sickly; Bevin and Cripps were to die within the year. The determination to battle on seems not to have existed. Instead there was an acceptance that another election was likely in the near future, and that contentious legislation should be avoided. The Korean War and Britain's commitment dominated this short administration, and Bevan's resignation provided the excitement. The 1951 election was fought on Labour's domestic record – rising prices and continuing shortages, especially housing – and on Churchill's accusation that the socialists levelled down and that Nye Bevan was a communist plotting to undermine Attlee and capture the party. Not all these barbs hit home. As in 1950, the curiosities of the British political system enabled Labour to garner 48.8 per cent of the votes compared with the Conservatives 48 per cent and still win 26 fewer seats than their rivals (295 to 321). Churchill returned to office. Labour departed to spend 13, often bitterly divided, years in opposition.

1. The Realities of Labour's Inheritance in 1945

(a) A lot of people envisaged the Labour government's victory as going to build a new world at long term. A lot of other people envisaged it as an opportunity to get back on the results of a great deal of Tory rule. But, in fact, by far the most pressing
5 and dominant item on the agenda was to reconstruct the war industry of this country; to redeploy the labour force to enable us to earn our keep in the quite hideous situation which arose from the sudden cut-off of American aid. We had sold most of our foreign investment. We had no export products nor export
10 markets to replace these overseas earnings; and suddenly, almost overnight, by Congressional decision all this aid, which had been enabling us to live while we were fighting for the allied cause and while we were taking a disproportionate share of the war burden, was cut off. We were in a most extraordin-
15 ary position then, but theoretically we were one of the most powerful countries on earth. As time went on it became clear that whatever grandiose ideas people might have, it was the bread and butter jobs of getting those demobbed people into industry earning our keep in exports, export or die, all this
20 productivity campaign, this bread and butter stuff, that was more, much more, important. In the early part of the Attlee administration, there were problems of just taking to bits various war-time controls, of finding out what controls, what rationing, for instance, would have to continue, so as to enable
25 us to make a transition to peace time. All this was occupying the foreground of the agenda for ministers and the Civil Service in a way which I think was never perhaps fully understood in other circles. It was a dominant issue just to live day by day in order to come out of it in a position where Britain could have
30 the rewards which everyone felt that, having won the war, they were entitled to.

> Max Nicholson, Secretary of Office of Lord President of the
> Council 1945–52, interviewed by Thames Television, sum-
> mer 1970.

(b) Keynes's brilliance rather alarmed the Americans. I think they were wary of it; and in a curious sort of way if he'd been a less brilliant negotiator, we might have had a better result. On the American side there was not at that time the realization of the
5 extent to which the war had impoverished Europe and had drained the resources of the United Kingdom. That realization didn't come until later, when the Americans turned from giving priority to their relations with the Russians, to giving priority to the reconstruction of Western Europe. Therefore,
10 since they were not aware of the full extent of the problem, the

loan which was eventually negotiated was really too small and
the conditions were too stringent – for example, the conditions
that sterling should be made convertible. On the British side
there was a great reluctance to accept the loan, particularly on
15   these conditions. Of course, the American negotiators had to
keep a very wary eye on Congress, which was also very
reluctant to give even this degree of assistance to the United
Kingdom.

> Lord Sherfield, Deputy Under Secretary in the Foreign
> Office 1948–52, interviewed by Thames Television, sum-
> mer 1970.

Both extracts were printed in Alan Thompson, *The Day before
Yesterday*, Sidgwick & Jackson, 1971, p. 24.

Questions

Extract (a)
a What, according to Max Nicholson, was 'the most pressing and
dominant item on the agenda' (lines 4–5)?
b What were the implications of the 'Congressional decision'
(line 11)?
c What decision had to be made by the Attlee administration 'to
enable us to make a transition to peace time' (lines 24–5)?

Extract (b)
a Over what did Keynes have to negotiate (lines 1–3) in 1945?
b What did the Americans fail to realise about Europe and the
United Kingdom and why?
c Why was the loan eventually extracted from America the object
of suspicion on both sides of the Atlantic?
d When and why did American suspicion evaporate after 1945?

2. Devaluation

The decisive point of the 1949 devaluation was the meeting with
the Commonwealth Finance Ministers in the first week of July,
when it became quite apparent, if you compared the export price of
British goods with those of American goods in all the main export
5   markets of the world, that American prices were 25 per cent or 30
per cent on average below ours, which really was conclusive
evidence that you couldn't maintain that rate of exchange. Strangely
enough, the man who really produced the clearest and most
decisive evidence was Sir Edgar Whitehead, the then Finance
10   Minister of Southern Rhodesia and who later became Prime
Minister of Southern Rhodesia.

There was a seething ferment of disagreement within the Treasury: broadly, the economists were convinced that it was necessary. I was economic secretary and the senior civil servants naturally took the more cautious view. I think they were quite right to do this, it's a very drastic step. Stafford Cripps, characteristically, took rather a long view of the whole thing: that this just wasn't the sort of thing that one did, and he didn't really quite frankly, fully understand the argument for it. This went on, I would say, for a couple of weeks. I came to the conclusion on the third Sunday in July that devaluation was necessary. Hugh Gaitskell and I and Harold Wilson had been made responsible for economic policy under the Prime Minister when Stafford Cripps was away. He was leaving for Switzerland on the Monday. I therefore went round and saw Hugh Gaitskell on the morning of that Monday. I told him the conclusion I had come to and that we must get on with it. He at once said that he had come to the same conclusion on exactly the same day, for exactly the same reasons. So I told Stafford Cripps just before lunch before he went that I wasn't arguing the thing but I ought in fairness to tell him I had come to this conclusion. He said 'What – unilaterally?' and was, I remember, very shocked. That was all he said. And then there were discussions in the remaining week – the last week before the dispersal of Parliament and usually the last cabinet meeting until September – between Hugh Gaitskell, myself, Harold Wilson, the Treasury officials, and Attlee and Morrison. And by the end of that week they were convinced that there was no alternative. I mean Attlee's view was always that he didn't profess to understand all these things but that it was the fact that the gold was disappearing. Therefore he rather left it at that and the cabinet was then asked to give authority to deal with the whole dollar problem, as we called it in those days, to the Prime Minister during the recess. And I remember that far from displaying any objections to this possibly rather authoritarian proposal, everybody heaved a sigh of relief. They were then told not to make any speeches about dollars or sterling throughout August and September. It was left at that. We then dispatched a very secret letter to Stafford Cripps in Zurich, which I drafted, as a matter of fact. Hugh Gaitskell and I took it down to Chequers, it was signed by Attlee and taken overnight to Stafford Cripps. Stafford gave a rather reluctant assent. Preparations then went ahead. I think it was the most successful operation I've ever seen carried out in Whitehall, because there was no leak of any kind. The date was set and Stafford Cripps and Ernie Bevin went out to the International Monetary Fund meeting in September just the day after.

Douglas Jay, Labour MP and Economic Secretary to the Treasury 1946 to 1950, interviewed on Thames Television, 1970, and printed in Alan Thompson, *The Day before Yesterday*, Sidgwick & Jackson, 1971, p. 64.

a What for Douglas Jay, was the 'conclusive evidence that you couldn't maintain that rate of exchange' (lines 6–7)?

b Summarise the disagreement over the issue within the Treasury.

c How did Attlee choose to deal with the problem?

d Why might this have been considered a particularly sensitive issue for those Labour politicians with long memories and a sense of history?

3. Nationalisation of Coal

(a) I was asked by Attlee to go to the Ministry of Fuel and Power with a seat in the cabinet and to nationalize the mines. He also asked me to nationalize the electric supply and gas. I went back to my department, consulted with my Permanent Under-Secretary and
5 other officials, and they said to me 'Well, you'll have to prepare the headings, Minister'. Naturally, I looked around for some information, for blue-prints, but there were none in the department. I went to the Labour Party; there was very little there. There was a pamphlet written by Arthur Greenwood, who was a very
10 prominent member of the Labour Party. There were several resolutions passed at the Labour Party conference, no blue-prints, so I had to tackle it as if it was something quite new. It was very difficult indeed to do it.

The coal industry was pretty bad at the time because it had
15 been neglected during the war. Thousands of men had left the pits either to go into the Forces or to enter the munitions industries, and the industry was completely neglected; it was in a terrible state. Meanwhile, industrial production was increasing at a rapid rate and demands were made for more coal as
20 there were more demands for more electricity supply. You can imagine the nature of the problem. I couldn't say very much about it. I was very optimistic about the situation: the miners' leaders had promised to produce the coal. When we had nationalised the industry, of course, all sorts of problems
25 presented themselves (shortage of labour, shortage of equipment) and so there was trouble. In addition to which we had trouble on the railways. Then there was some trouble about production and we weren't able to produce the stuff. We found that we couldn't get it to the people who wanted it. So
30 nationalization, although it had been advocated over so many years and regarded as one of the most substantial items of the Labour party programme, wasn't altogether a success.

LORD SHINWELL

(b) The Labour movement made a fundamental error when, from time to time, almost with monotonous regularity at its annual conference, it moved resolutions to nationalize something or another but did nothing about it; there was no real research done on how you would organize a publicly owned enterprise of this size. The result was, by and large, that the nationalization acts were based upon work that had been done very largely by others and in the main by people who did not share the ideas of nationalization. The coal industry, for example, was based on the work of Sir Charles Reed, who was in fact employed by the coal owners and paid by the coal owners to do a complete survey of the coal industry and produce a scheme for rationalization. Indeed Sir Charles Reed became an original member of the National Coal Board.
LORD ROBENS

> Lord Shinwell, Minister of Fuel and Power 1945–7, and Lord Robens, Parliamentary Secretary to the Ministry of Fuel and Power 1947–51, interviewed by Thames Television 1970 and printed in Alan Thompson, *The Day before Yesterday*, Sidgwick & Jackson, 1971, p. 26.

Questions

Using Both Extracts
a In what state of preparation were Labour plans for nationalization in 1945?

Using Extract (a)
b What was 'the nature of the problem' (line 21) which faced Shinwell in the coal industry before and after nationalization?
c 'I was very optimistic about the situation' (line 22). Why was Shinwell's optimism at the centre of considerable controversy and the cause of much embarrassment in February 1947?
d Would you agree with Shinwell that nationalization (of coal) 'wasn't altogether a success' (line 32)?
e How reliable is the testimony of this interview, recorded in 1970, by Lord Shinwell?

Using Extract (b)
f What was the consequence of this state of preparation for the structure and management of the nationalized coal industry?

4. Reasons for Nationalisation

When a private monopoly control reaches the magnitude of that in the iron and steel industry, and thereby the power to influence the strategic requirements of the State and the interests of a large

proportion of our main industries, it is not right, in my view, that
it should be perpetuated. Parliament must be able to supervise this
vital section of our industry in the interests of the nation and of the
consumer. In other words, the time has come when the size,
importance and structure of the steel industry demands the change
from private to public monopoly control. It is not a question as
between uncontrolled private enterprise and national ownership. . . . but between the private or public control of a vital
industry. . . .

This leads me to the second point, which is that, now we are
seeking to have some measure of foresight in our economic
activities, we must be able, so far as certain basic matters are
concerned, to plan ahead for production. The whole of our capital
investment programme, of our programme for investment overseas, including that in our overseas territories – which is a large part
of our export business – depend upon supplies of suitable qualities
of steel, and we must be able to plan this most important of our
economic activities ahead; and that we certainly cannot do if we are
to be driven to rely upon the reactions of uncontrolled private
enterprise to a changing world situation in which they may demand
again the restriction of markets, high prices, international cartel
agreements, tariffs, and import restrictions as a condition of
making the necessary supplies available to the country.

We cannot allow the steel industry to determine, from the point
of view of nothing but its own profitability, the limits of its own
expansion. The only entity that can take the risk, in the present
highly speculative circumstances of world economy, as to the
future size and form of the steel industry that we can build up, is the
nation as a whole. . . .

The third point is the strategic one. We cannot again, as we did
before the last war, leave it to the chances of the interests of private
enterprise to determine whether or not we shall have adequate
capacity suitably located to provide our defence needs. Just as in the
early days of our sea power it was found essential to the national
safety for the State to own and run some naval dockyards, so today
it is essential for our defence needs that the State should own a large
part of the steel-making resources of the country so that they can be
assured that the defence position is always safeguarded. . . .

There has been too much experience in past times of the misuse
of industrial power and of the essential resources of the nation
owing to reliance upon the unrestrained operation of the law of
supply and demand in association with the equally unrestrained
operation of the profit motive. These are, of course, essential
factors in our mixed economic activities, but more and more the
people demand that they should be brought under reasonable
control to ensure that national resources are used in the interests of
the people as a whole, and not to increase the wealth and power of

any particular section of the population. This Bill is a step forward in that direction, and will serve to establish that our democratic processes are capable of dealing with the most deeply entrenched sectors of private enterprise, as and when it is in the nation's
55 interest that such action shall be taken.

> From a speech in the House of Commons by Sir Stafford Cripps, *Hansard*, 16 November 1948, c 458, 319, 321–41, 324.

Questions

a What is Cripps's first reason for ensuring that 'Parliament supervise this vital section of our industry' (lines 6–7)?

b In what ways does Cripps, in the second paragraph of the passage, see private enterprise as antipathetical to the new goals of Labour's economic management where 'now we are seeking to have some measure of foresight in our economic activities' (lines 13–15)?

c What is Cripps's 'strategic' point (line 33)?

d Why, unlike coal, gas, electricity and the railways was iron and steel nationalization a bitterly contended issue, both within the Labour Party and between Labour and Conservatives?

5. Bevin in Perspective

Bevin's ultimate purpose was to give Labour a credible stance in international affairs. From its earlier history, and especially from the thirties, Labour had inherited a confused bundle of sensations, socialist, populist, neo-pacifist, anti-imperialist, deeply suspicious
5 of reality and power in world affairs. Despite the change in the later thirties and the reassessments brought about by the war, these confusions were still far from resolved in July 1945. Many voices then, within the party and outside, called, with more passion than precision, for 'a socialist foreign policy'. This idea, however
10 ambiguous, did register the genuine belief that the 1945 election would mean a revolution in Britain's foreign as well as its domestic policy, after the shameful pre-war record of the right-wing appeasers. Labour came to the Foreign Office, in that sense, with clean hands. Bevin fuelled popular hopes by emphasising, in a
15 much misquoted passage, that 'left understands left'. But his move to the Foreign Office soon resulted in calls for a 'socialist foreign policy' – especially when made by such an erratic figure as Richard Crossman, who by 1949 had totally recanted – being exposed as the empty and unrealistic rhetoric it really was.
20   Bevin's outlook was crucial because Britain in July 1945 manifestly felt itself to be a great power. Britain's post-war decline, like

Mark Twain's death, is often exaggerated. Britain was one of the 'big three' who had won the war. It had immense world-wide commitments unique among the nations – strategic, financial, and
25 geographical in the Middle East above all, but also in the Far East, Australasia, throughout Africa, north and south and in the Caribbean. It was easily the ascendant nation in western Europe, the one major power Hitler had never been able to invade. Of course, Britain's position was in many ways based on an illusion kept alive
30 – especially as regards its financial strength – by such false aids as the sterling balances. The US loan of December 1945 was vitally necessary not only to maintain Britain's world-wide military and naval pretensions, but even to keep the essentials of Labour's programme at home in being.
35 Bevin's handling of this illusory position, as Alan Bullock describes it, went through three main phases. There was a period of uncertainty and frustration down to the late spring of 1947, with endless deadlock in negotiations with the Russians and much acrimony in the Council of Foreign Ministers. There were no
40 results to show, apart from the clear evidence of British economic weakness, revealed in successive decisions in early 1947 to withdraw from Greece, India and Palestine. Bevin's bugle note of advance covered a saga of imperial retreat. The merger of the British and US zones in Germany, the 'bizone' of January 1947,
45 was also partly the result of Britain's manifest economic difficulties in feeding and running its own zone of occupation. Then there followed the astonishing phase of achievement and diplomatic triumph of, roughly, June 1947 to May 1949, noted earlier. Finally, there came a time of consolidation and of renewed challenge,
50 symbolized by the outbreak of the Korean War in June 1950. Bevin's policy especially in terms of the Anglo-American relationship and the future of western European defence arrangements, was still in some flux at the time of his death.

But his legacy stood the test of time: much of it still provides the
55 parameters of our contemporary world. For historians of the British labour movement, Bevin's time at the Foreign Office is fascinating for the transformation in attitudes it implied. For a party long pacifist in its instincts, it meant a long-term policy of high defence expenditure, military conscription in peacetime, and
60 even the covert commitment to Britain's possession of nuclear weapons on an independent basis. For a movement deeply anti-German ('I regard them all as Huns', Dalton sagely observed in 1951), it meant a political settlement with Germany and the gradual association of the Federal Republic with the political and defence
65 strategies of the democratic western nations. Hopes that German steel barons would be nationalized into oblivion were set aside, partly under US pressure. For a party of 'little Englanders' (including many Welsh and Scots), it meant a new involvement of Britain

with the defence and security arrangements of continental Europe
70 for the rest of the century, as embodied in the Brussels Treaty of
March 1948. And, for men and women sometimes moved by an
almost Pavlovian hostility to capitalist America and the omnipo-
tence of Wall Street, it meant a lasting commitment to a military
and economic alliance with the United States, dating from early
75 collaboration in facing up to Stalin during the Iran crisis of 1945–6,
through the forming of the German 'bizone' and the later conception of the Marshall Plan, down to the military arrangements of
NATO, and the economic collaboration of OEEC and the European Recovery Programme. The spectre of a return to US isola-
80 tionism was dispelled for ever.

Most shattering of all, for British socialists committed to a
sentimental tenderness for fellow socialist regimes from 1917
onwards, a feeling rekindled by the victories of the Red Army
during the war, it implied a stern, unrelenting hostility to the
85 Soviet Union.

The view expressed by the British Ambassador, Sir Oliver
Franks, in June 1950, that Britain had achieved a unique international influence since 1947 through the interlocking special relationship to the United States, its headship of the sterling area and the
90 Commonwealth and its lead in western Europe, could have com-
manded the general assent of most of the British labour movement
at that time.

> From Kenneth O. Morgan, *Labour People*, Oxford Univer-
> sity Press, 1987, pp. 154–6.

Questions

a What do you understand by the term (line 16) 'socialist foreign
   policy'?
b To what extent did Bevin's foreign policy reveal Britain's
   inherent weakness after the end of the war?
c In what ways did Bevin reshape traditional Labour attitudes in
   foreign policy?
d How would you assess Bevin's achievement as Foreign Secretary between 1945–50?

6. Keep Left's Socialist Foreign Policy

We cannot expect that the tension between Russia and America will
be reduced in the immediate future, and we shall probably have to
plan on the assumption that no agreement between them is likely
for some time either on the control of atomic energy or on
5 large-scale disarmament. It will be an uneasy and dangerous sort of
world.

In these conditions one thing is clear. No European nation will be any safer for taking shelter in either an anti-American or an anti-Russian bloc. The security of each and of all of us depends on preventing the division of Europe into exclusive spheres of influence.

It is here that Britain, working as closely as possible with France, can take the lead. Our immediate aim should be a joint Anglo-French declaration formally abjuring Staff conversations either with the USA or with the USSR. We should make it clear that our joint defence plans will be framed within a regional European security system, according to the terms of the United Nations' Charter, and be designed to deter aggression either by Germany or by any non-European Power. Such a declaration would do something to reduce the Russian suspicion that Western Europe is being used for the preparation of war against the Soviet Union.

We should try to expand the Anglo-French Alliance into a European security pact, and announce our readiness, along with other European nations, to renounce the manufacture and use of atomic bombs and to submit our armed forces and armament factories to inspection of UNO, irrespective of whether Russia and America reach agreement on this subject or not. This involves no sacrifice of security for us, since our security depends not on winning the next – atomic – war, but on preventing it. A United Europe, strong enough to deter an aggressor, but voluntarily renouncing the most deadly offensive weapon of modern warfare, would be the best guarantor of world peace.

The greatest obstacle to European unity is, of course, the German problem. Both Russia and America secretly fear German unity. Russia fears that a united Germany could be used as an anti-communist bulwark against her. America is equally afraid of a Communist Germany. France, not unnaturally, is obsessed by her own weakness *vis-à-vis* a united Germany. . . .

The German problem remains insoluble so long as Europe remains divided. Our primary aim, therefore, must be to find a way of reconciling the French demand for security with the economic necessity for an end of zonal administration in Germany. To condemn the Potsdam Agreement and attempt to fix a level of production for German industry is not sufficient. Potsdam must be replaced by an agreement compatible with Europe's needs.

Such an agreement can be based only on the integration of German economy into that of her neighbours. As we have seen, every European state is now developing its own national plan. The plan for German reconstruction must be fitted into these national plans and into the five-year plan of Soviet Russia, and they in turn must be co-ordinated with each other.

From R. H. S. Crossman, Michael Foot and Ian Mikardo, 'Keep Left', April 1947, pp. 38, 40–41, printed in F. Bealey (ed.) *The Social and Political Thought of the British Labour Party*, Weidenfeld & Nicolson, 1970, pp. 170–1.

Questions

a From your reading of lines 1 to 32, summarise the main principles of 'Keep Left's' foreign policy.

b In what ways did this challenge official Labour policy as enunciated and practised by Bevin and Attlee?

c What parallels can you find between the ideas for 'a European security pact. . . . submi[ssion of] our armed forces and armament factories to inspection of UNO' (lines 23–6) and the policies of Labour in the 1920s and 1930s?

d What was 'Keep Left's' policy for the solution of the German problem? (lines 33–51)? In what ways was it visionary in relation to what actually happened after 1950?

e Why might the phrase 'voluntarily renouncing the most deadly offensive weapon of modern warfare' (lines 30–1) have been unintentionally ironic when applied to British official policy in 1947?

7.   Labour and the Bomb

Attlee has been much criticised for coming to that decision: it is said that he should have foreseen that the 'independent deterrent' would be impossibly expensive and would never be independent, since it could never be used unless the Americans agreed to its use. In the
5 late 1950s its existence threatened to split the Labour Party, brought about the leftwing-led Campaign for Nuclear Disarmament, and precipitated the demonstrations and protests for unilateral nuclear disarmament which caused much turbulence in Anglo-American relations.
10   A judgement on Attlee for giving the word for Britain to manufacture her own atomic bomb should take into account the circumstances in which he had to make the decision. In the first days of 1947 the Russians were strongly entrenched in Europe. The 'Truman Doctrine' of containment of the Russians was in its
15 infancy. There was a possibility that the presidential election of the following year would result in the election of an isolationist Republican who would withdraw the American presence from Europe, leaving Britain to resist further expansion of the Russians to the west. Britain could not have resisted the Russian advance
20 with conventional weapons. It is therefore not surprising that the chiefs of staff asked for the British bomb. A prime minister would have taken a great risk if he had decided to refuse their request.
    Attlee had no doubts about it:

'If we had decided not to have it, we would have put ourselves
25 entirely in the hands of the Americans. That would have been a risk
a British government should not take. It's all very well to look
back, and to say otherwise, but at that time nobody could be sure
that the Americans would not revert to isolationism – many
Americans feared it. There was no NATO then. For a power of our
30 size and with our responsibilities to turn its back on the Bomb did
not make sense.'

This was the general consensus. Professor Gowing concludes:

'The British decision to make an atomic bomb had 'emerged' from
a body of general assumptions. It had not been a response to an
35 immediate military threat but rather something fundamentalist and
almost instinctive – a feeling that Britain must possess so climacteric
a weapon in order to deter an atomically armed enemy, a feeling
that Britain as a great power must acquire all major new weapons, a
feeling that atomic weapons were a manifestation of the scientific
40 and technological superiority on which Britain's strength, so
deficient if measured in sheer numbers of men, must depend.'

From *Attlee*, by Kenneth Harris, Weidenfeld & Nicolson,
1982, pp. 288–9.

Questions

a   What criticisms have been levelled at Attlee for his decision to
invest in the 'independent deterrent' (line 3)?
b   Why, according to Harris, are the circumstances in which he
had to make the decision (lines 11–12) important in making a
judgement?
c   Of what 'fundamentalist and almost instinctive' response (lines
35–6) does Professor Gowing talk in explaining Britain's decision to make a bomb?
★ d   Why did this issue become so contentious for the Labour Party,
both in the 1950s and in the 1980s?

8. The Palestine Problem

The Americans simply said 'You take all those Jews to Palestine
and you look after them, and you take all the consequences from
the Arabs. That will reduce the number of Jews who will come to
America'. I've never seen a more selfish attitude than the American
5 government adopted. I must say, here I sympathize with Bevin
because it was insupportable. The American government's attitude
was self-righteous. They said 'It's your job to look after all the
survivors of the concentration camps, you take them all into
Palestine. After all, when you ask the Jews now at least as many of

10   them wanted to go to the States as wanted to go to Palestine'. But
there was a quota into the States and did the Americans lift the
quota? Not one iota. So there was fury – I can understand Bevin
and Attlee being angry with Truman for lecturing to them. They
had to do all this without American help because the Americans
15   would not help us at all at the time, and were not concerned to go
into the Middle East. The other American attitude, of course,
which made it particularly irritating to the British, was that the
Jews were seen as being true Americans fighting George III and that
this was the American revolution all over again. Ernie Bevin was
20   regarded really as George III incarnate today, with all his wicked-
ness. Now it was a bit irritating to a Labour government to be
treated in this way by an American Democratic President. . . .

I think, frankly, at the beginning there was no anti-Semitism. At
the beginning, Ernie Bevin was a natural Englishman, and there-
25   fore of course a natural anti-Semite. But Bevin only became
anti-Semitic when he found that the Jews were frustrating him. By
the end of his life he was, in one sense of the word, ravingly
anti-Semitic, dangerously so. But it was something which grew on
him as the result of the situation. The Jews wouldn't fit in with his
30   plan to hold the Middle East, to hold the oil. For that he needed a
Suez base. For the Suez base he needed a friendly Palestine, a
friendly Palestine meant to him an Arab Palestine with an acquie-
scent Jewish minority and the Jews said they wouldn't acquiesce, so
they had to be broken. I must say he was pretty rough from the
35   start. You will remember when he said, right at the beginning of
1945, that 'you shouldn't shove to the head of the queue'. But to
poor people who'd just had 6,000,000 people murdered in concentration camps, it wasn't the most tactful way of addressing the
survivors, to say this kind of thing. But it was only, as I say,
40   something coming out of him. He was a very primitive man in
certain ways, enormously powerful, able, but with a simple
brutality at the bottom which was combined with a great buoyancy
and a great kindness so you had both brutality and kindness in him.
He simply couldn't stand his sense of frustration. The Jews were
45   deeply shocked by this brutal and simple man and they under-
estimated him. They saw him at his worst – at his bullying worst.

Richard Crossman, Labour MP in 1945, interviewed in 1970
for Thames Television, and published in Alan Thompson,
The Day before Yesterday, Sidgwick & Jackson, 1971, p. 37.

Questions

a   What was the attitude of the Americans to the Palestine problem? Why was this so?
b   Why, according to Crossman, did Bevin become anti-Semitic?
c   Why were Bevin and the Foreign Office Arabist in outlook?

d It has been said of Bevin that, over Palestine, 'he was caught between a rock and a hard place'. To what extent was he making policy in an impossible situation between 1945 and 1948? What were the results of his policy for Palestine in 1948–9?

9. Bevan and the National Health Service

If he was to have a universal health service – making the best available to all – he needed the top doctors and patients at least partly inside it. If he could only have this by leaving them the option of private practice, so be it; he believed that, once all were
5 inside, the superiority of the NHS would become evident and private practice would wither away.... A doctrinaire attempt to impose the SMA's (Socialist Medical Association) integrated service based on the local authority hospitals and health centres, with the doctors employed by the local authorities, might have
10 been the 'correct' (socialist) solution on paper, but it would have meant a two-tier system in practice because so many of the top doctors and their patients would have opted out....

The BMA declared itself content and on the 'Appointed Day' attempted to take for itself as much as possible of the credit for the
15 new Service.

Paradoxically, of course, it was entitled to do so: for it was arguably more responsible than any other body for the final shape and limitations of the NHS. It was, after all, the doctors' rejection of the Ministry of Health's original ideas, based on local authority
20 health centres linked to local authority hospitals, which had created by 1945 the deadlock from which Bevan escaped by nationalising the hospitals while leaving the general practitioner service, as the general practitioners wanted, essentially undisturbed. All the most fundamental criticism, made at the time and since, of the structure
25 of the NHS as set up in 1948 can be traced back to the decision not to base the service on the local authorities. The various medical services, it is argued, were fragmented instead of unified, and the gulf between the GPs and the hospitals widened instead of closed; there was no provision for preventive medicine, only treatment;
30 there was inadequate financial discipline, and no democratic control below the power ultimately vested in the Minister. All these things are true....

Bevan's primary achievement, which no amount of criticism can take away from him is that he was the Minister who set the Service
35 up; after years of talking, it fell to him to take the key decisions, draft and carry the Bill through Parliament and administer the immense job of creating the machinery and appointing all the necessary Boards and committees to run it. This, as a new Minister

40 with no previous experience, he did with remarkable efficiency and
flair. He delivered the new Service to the nation. His secondary
achievement, however, was to contrive the appearance of a political
triumph for his party when in fact he had enacted virtually none of
the cherished nostrums of those in the Labour Party who had cared
about health.

45 For the most part the leaders of the SMA fell in with the general
mood, swallowed their criticisms and hailed the NHS as their own.
But the one idea that in 1948 they still hoped had been saved from
the wreck of their original vision was the concept of the health
centre. Throughout the passage of the legislation, both in the
50 wording of the Bill and in his exposition of it, Bevan had laid great
stress on the importance attached to health centres; their provision
would be a duty on the local authorities, and though of course no
doctor would be obliged to work in them, their development
would be 'encouraged in every possible way'. In time, it was still
55 possible for the SMA to believe the health centres would be the
means of reforming the GP service, keeping alive the possibility of
group practice and salaries, and overcoming the fragmentation of
the NHS as a whole. In practice, however, as Bevan wearing his
other hat as Minister of Housing knew only too well, there were no
60 resources available for building centres; and in fact none were built
until the 1960s. . . .

But Bevan had never been committed to the doctrinaire SMA
prescription. His idea of socialised medicine centred rather on the
two principles of universality and free treatment – the extension on
65 a national scale of the rights offered by the Tredegar Medical Aid
Society in his youth. How the treatment was delivered he was
content to regard as a matter of administration which he was not
prepared to make a point of principle. In 1948 he had secured most
of what he wanted from a national health service.

> From J. Campbell, *Nye Bevan and the Mirage of Socialism*,
> Weidenfeld & Nicolson, 1987, pp. 168–9, 177–9.

Questions

a   How did Bevan's National Health Service reflect socialist thinking on health reform?
b   Why was it 'paradoxical' (line 16) that the BMA was 'arguably
more responsible than any other body for the final shape and
limitation of the NHS' (lines 17–18)?
c   What 'fundamental criticisms' have been made about the structure of the NHS since its inception? (line 24)
d   What was Bevan's role in the creation of the NHS?
e   What socialist concept did the SMA still hope to save 'from the
wreck of their original vision' (lines 47–8) and how committed
was Bevan to it?

f What were the fundamental principles of Bevan's conception of a national health service? How far have they been perpetuated down to the present day?